GIFTS OF AGE

CHRONICLE BOOKS

GIFTS OF AGE

Portraits and Essays
of 32 Remarkable Women

For Susan,
Best Wishes,
Pamela Valois
July 1991

Text by Charlotte Painter · Photography by Pamela Valois

Hear her, therefore, as the latest voice;
The intervening generations (drifting
On tides of fancy still), ignore.

Robert Graves
from "The Great-Grandmother"

Acknowledgments

Many people have helped with the project, and we wish to thank them for their support: Carolyn Robertson for her help in the planning stages; Linda Spector of the College Avenue Players; Suzanne Riess and the Regional Oral History Project of the Bancroft Library for their help in research; the campus of DQU; Florence Jury; Maggie Gee; Lois Oaks; Robbin Henderson; Laurie Shields; Linden Berry; Mary Kent; Peggy Love; Margaretta Mitchell; Ronald Barnes; Nell Altizer; Mary Jane Moffat; Sherry Burkart; Mary Beth Whittemore; Barbara Traisman; Susan Kanaan; our agent, Martha Casselman; and our editor, Barbara Youngblood. We are grateful to all the women who appear in these pages and who shared their stories with such generosity and candor.

Special thanks are due to Lloyd Linford, Pamela Valois's husband, for his constant moral support and editorial help throughout the project.

Copyright © 1985 by Charlotte Painter and Pamela Valois.

"The Great-Grand Mother" by Robert Graves is quoted by permission of the Robert Graves estate.

Printed in Japan by Toppan Printing Co., Ltd., Tokyo

Library of Congress Cataloging in Publication Data:

Painter, Charlotte.
    Gifts of age.

    1. Aged women—California. 2. Aged women—California —Portraits. 3. Minority women—California. 4. Minority women—California—Portraits. I. Title.
HQ1064.U6C354 1985   305.4'09794   85-13267
ISBN 0-87701-368-3 (pbk.)

Distributed in Canada by Raincoast Books, 112 East Third Avenue, Vancouver, B.C. V5T 1C8

15   14   13   12   11   10   9   8

Editing: Barbara Youngblood
Composition: On Line
Book and cover design: Linda Herman

Chronicle Books
275 Fifth Street
San Francisco, CA 94103

Contents

A Note by the Photographer

Several years ago I read an essay by Elizabeth Janeway, "Breaking the Age Barrier," in which she speaks of our need to overcome the stereotypes of aging, which are based on the sick and needy rather than on the healthy and fulfilled. At the time I knew one remarkable older woman, my photography teacher, Ruth Bernhard. She was in her late sixties, and a number of us met with her regularly each month for critiques. During this period, I realized I needed an experienced woman friend to help me understand the problems I would face in midlife—how to balance a career with my friendships and family and how to further my own personal development while being involved with motherhood. I found myself studying Ruth to see how she managed such things in her own life. In contrast to the stereotypes, she seemed to grow *more* vigorous each year into her seventies.

Then I got to know my landlady and neighbor, Jacomena Maybeck. My husband and I felt fortunate to be renting a house she owned, a magical, rambling cottage in the Berkeley hills. Shortly after moving in, I went out and found her, barefoot, dressed in a halter top and shorts, energetically sloshing tar over leaky spots on the roof of her house. She was seventy-eight at the time. I realized that no stereotype of older women could account for Jackie. We became great friends. My relationship with her is the inspiration for this book.

A widow, Jacomena has a career in ceramics and has introduced me to many active and interesting women in their seventies and eighties. I began to think about what these women meant to me and why I was so drawn to them. Their relationships with others appeared to me deeper, more enduring than those of younger people I knew. These older women have continued to change and develop. I found them democratic, spontaneous, open to new experiences.

As a photographer, I set out to build a collective portrait of these women. I hoped that some of their character might come through in their postures, their gestures, their faces and expressions. I asked men and women my own age if they knew older people I might photograph and was surprised that many friends had someone special they wanted me to meet.

As my work progressed, I became much more optimistic about my own old age. The women spoke of advantages and privileges they found in these years. My new relationships with older women have affected me on many levels, including my dream life. For years I've had the troubling, recurrent dream of having to go back to college, only to find there's no space for me in the dormitory. In a recent dream, though, I discovered an old building on the edge of campus with a Rooms for Rent sign in front. When I entered and took the elevator to the top, I was shown into a large, glassed-in game room. To my great surprise there were twenty old women hand-wrestling and tumbling about on the floor. They were having a marvelous time and invited me to join in.

It goes without saying that not all of us will gain admission to that room, but perhaps our chances can be increased if we free ourselves from stereotypical thinking and actually get to know older people we admire.

Pamela Valois

PREFACE

I was touched by these photographs when Pamela Valois showed them to me, as much by Pamela herself as by the pictures. The mother of two small children, she was too young and attractive to be concerned about aging, I thought. That was more a problem for someone in her middle years, like myself. Avoidance was my program, as I suspect it is for many others. I soon saw that Pamela didn't look upon her quest as a "problem," but rather as a way of praising her friends and teachers. And so I began to learn.

I went to visit the women she had photographed, as well as a few others as my enthusiasm for the project grew. I asked each of them to tell me a story about her life in the later years. Some of the stories they told I've written as sketches or vignettes. To an artist a vignette is a picture with no definite border that shades off at the edges. That idea kept coming to me as I wrote, because of an attitude of mind in many of the women themselves. Their lives are filled with rare imagery, some of it quite small in size but often shimmering with beauty. Virgina Woolf called such imagery "moments of being"—when a shock causes the cotton wool of ordinary existence to fall away from reality itself, to reveal richness and meaning.

A group of writers composed largely of men with whom I meet regularly gave me an insight into this view of life. When I told them about this book, they became somewhat sad, as if I were entering a delicate, almost ghostly realm, where there was much that might not be spoken of. Death and old age felt synonymous to them. One suggested I ask each woman to talk to me about her mother's death as a way of edging up on the subject of her own. It struck me that these men saw life in a linear fashion and that old age for them was the end of a line leading straight to the grave.

This was not the response I found among the women themselves; to them the grave does not loom straight ahead. Rather they spoke about living as part of a cyclic process and of death as part of that cycle of life. There was a feeling of a spiral toward knowledge and of wholeness, completion, the way a circle is complete. There was anxiety about the prospect of ill health and frailty. A universal dread is the nursing home, but I found very little fear of death. Rather there was a strong desire to live as long as health and functioning last. These women expressed an enormous joie de vivre, interest, excitement, adventurousness, passion.

At eighty-two the analyst Florida Scott-Maxwell wrote in her journal that she felt more passionate in her later years than ever before. Her diary offers insight, too, into the nature of a woman's attitude toward death. She wrote that in her old age she believed her psyche had become complete, and yet there were times she felt she was scarcely here at all. She remembered her pregnancies: in the last months the child seemed to claim almost all of her body, leaving her uncertain as to whether her life was her own. She asked, "Is life a pregnancy? That would make death a birth." Perhaps biology determines our attitudes throughout the whole of life.

These women support Scott-Maxwell's thinking. We saw Margaret Gardner enjoying a resonance with the cycles of her garden; we heard Ursula Casper speak of "dying" each day as a letting go for renewal of life; we listened to Martha St. John's advice to the lonely: they would not need others if they got in touch with the nurture of the earth itself.

M.F.K. Fisher told us she did not believe people changed in their later years, just became more of what they already were. Someone who was a bully as a child would be likely to become an old bully. That could be an expression of freedom, for the aged often give up hiding their worst nature, perhaps feeling they have nothing to lose. We found some women becoming free to act independently for the first time in old age. Previously held down by the demands of families and husbands, they were at last able to discover who they really are, and to remember what as children and young women they had liked to do. Anna Neilsen is studying poetry, history, philosophy—whatever she was unable to find time for in a married-working life; Alice Snyder is enjoying a conscious second childhood in a playful old age; Cecil Pierce, divorced late in life, has switched her work from seamstress to actress. M.F.K. Fisher herself has surely become more of what she has always been, an unequaled writer of personal narrative, whose work, even in her eighties, continues to astonish readers.

Robert Graves's poem "The Great-Grandmother" speaks of the candor of the aged ("confessions of old distaste") as a value we in the intervening generations owe it to ourselves to appreciate, for its truth is uncorrupted by "tides of fancy," ambition and worldliness.

As individuals become more of what they are in age, their ground of being suggests a multicolored variety as rich as the Grand Canyon's layers. Martha St. John speaks of the cultures of our country as blending, but at the same time urges young Native Americans to assume the burden of learning more than those in the dominant culture of plastic and technology in order to retain their individual tribal heritage. Lydia Feldschmidt's El Salvadoran roots spread tendrils of racial understanding in her good age. Frances Mary Albrier's commitment has flowered in benefits for blacks all over the country. The Asian women in the book, too, Haruko Obata and Alice Fong Yu, expressed a connection with their origins more passionate in age than ever before.

Common among all the women was a sense of faith. It takes as many forms as there are individuals. From Kay Seidell, a doctor, trained to a rational mode of thought, we heard an expression of belief in a soul, that understanding it was an unfinished task. At the other end of the spectrum, we found a committed spiritualist in Marie Lovejoy, who has a firm sense of contact with other planes of existence. There were churchgoers like Lucille Elliott, an analyst, also trained to rationalism, and Ada Perry, with faith in daily prayer. Although several expressed themselves as religious skeptics, they, too, are sustained by faith in life itself, in the young, in the human race, whatever its origins and destiny. Their practices, whether in arts, crafts, human relations, healing, or meditation, reflect that faith, a quality above all others that makes it exemplary appeal to those younger than they.

The last woman we interviewed, Tish Sommers, proved to be an ultimate confirmation to Pam Valois's impulse in focusing her art upon older women. In Tish we found not only a consummate activist, dedicated to the cause of the rights of elders through her organization the Older Women's League, but a woman whose faith, dedication, and charismatic qualities have given many younger women a sense of purpose, and even of adventurousness about aging.

My participation in this book was founded on a fear of aging that I became aware of when I first looked at the photographs. Writing about them would be a way of advancing toward what I fear, always the better part of valor, I believed. But as I progressed, I didn't find the enemy; I began to see that my fears themselves were cotton wool. The reality behind the wrinkles of these women became visible as a series of small shocks, each with its moment of enlightenment.

Demographic studies show us that the graying of America is an irreversible process as we live longer lives. We shall grow used to looking at older people, not only because they will become more numerous but because they will become more noticeable in what they do. These women can help us to undestand older people better and to realize that we can enjoy them enormously. They have learned to live in the moment, like true existentialists, released from the burden of the past and without fear of the future. Their faces are easy to look at, for they hold something that invites reflection. And in their hearts there is a lightness we might all emulate, and a grace.

Charlotte Painter

Jacomena Maybeck

Born March 19, 1901

Java is the birthplace of Jacomena May-beck, where her father was a sugar-refinery chemist; but when she was seven months old, her Dutch family went back to Holland. In her seventh year they moved permanently to California. Her father worked for the Spreckels refinery in Crockett, and the family lived on a ranch in Ukiah, where they became good friends with the Bernard Maybeck family. Maybeck had designed the Palace of Fine Arts in San Francisco and many romantic houses, with the broad redwood beams and high fireplaces for which he became famous.

Jacomena got to know his son, Wallen Maybeck, when she was only thirteen. After high school, she taught in a country school in Ukiah to save money for college; then she enrolled at the University of California at Berkeley in 1923.

The Maybecks had an empty studio and offered it to Jacomena and her brother, also in college. She remembers that all of their college friends used to gather on Sunday evenings with the elder Maybecks to listen to the "Standard Symphony" on the radio. There in the Berkeley hills, which were remote and forested in those days, her friendship with Wallen May-beck, who was an electrical engineer, deepened into a romance. They were married in 1927.

In the fifties, after their twin daughters had gone to college, Jacomena went to California College of Arts and Crafts for a master's degree, then taught ceramics there for many years.

She was widowed in 1964. Her family memoir, Maybeck, the Family View, *was published in 1979.*

PRIVILEGE

For quite a while she had needed a handrail to the house, some of her friends were very wobbly coming up the walk. Was the hill getting steeper? She couldn't just call a carpenter—a Maybeck house had to have just the right kind of railing.

Her potting kept her from taking care of it for a while. Funny thing about that creative impulse—from time to time she'd think, that's all over, I don't want to make anything anymore, it's dried up. Then she'd be wandering by a gallery, or she'd be caught by the shape of something, a rock or an animal, and the next thing she knew she was out in her pot shop fiddling around with the clay, letting the pieces come out. It was irrepressible, the desire to make things. She knew well enough not to worry when it went away now; it always came back, like a welcome friend. One privilege about being old was that she didn't have to worry about competition; a few years back she had felt obligated to make things that would look good in an exhibition. Now she just made things that seemed to want to get made, like this horse whose glaze she was finishing; blue and white he was, and bristling with his own energy.

Today she decided to do something about the railing. The time had come. She got on the phone to call the Boynton house. "Mr. Wonderful" was staying there, that blond, good-looking twenty-three-year-old visitor who could do anything.

The young man came over that afternoon to assess the problem. He took a tape measure out of his lean hip pocket, then together they went to the lumber supply store and bought some redwood two-by-fours and posts. It took no time to draw up the plans and put in the posts, but afterward she and Mr. Wonderful gazed at one another and shook their heads. It looked absolutely terrible.

"The only thing to do is to get something out of the woods," she said.

"I'll knock this right down," said Mr. Wonderful.

"Just leave the posts," she said. She went to the toolshed and took an ax. "Up this trail here," she said, and they set out.

Little Granny would have appreciated her care not to violate the house's design. Jacomena had learned to appreciate her mother-in-law more as the years went on, as she lived alone on this hill, realizing how numbered its days probably were. The few houses here on Maybeck Twin Drive were a little conservationist holdout, a treasure of how life used to be when artists first retreated to these hills. In a hundred years the hillside would be packed with condominiums, concrete blocks. Worse things would happen to these beloved hills than even Little Granny ever had imagined.

She thought of her mother-in-law often, and with affection, even though in life the old lady had made herself hard to love. "Dirty alcohol is never served in a Maybeck house, Jacomena." She hadn't wanted to harden against her, but neither had she wanted to melt down into this family and disappear. She had chosen to fight for the survival of her self.

"You are invited to this party, Mother, but Wallen and I are serving what pleases our guests."

The struggle was joined between the simple Dutch girl who had seemed so pliant, bred to a respect of elders, and the embattled woman intent upon her Calvinistic sense of propriety. Could Little Granny really have grasped the beauty of her own husband's architecture, which took its inspiration from an artist's longing for the remoteness of natural living among redwoods? The lofted ceilings of his houses might suggest cathedrals but never puritanism. Something in her must have known his houses were a response to the desire for freedom. Yet she herself could not be free.

For Little Granny there was too much error in the world, too much injustice to combat. Rare was the person who would cross the feisty little old lady on a stick in her battles over what was right for the hillside, for the community, for the family. Pride was her ruling passion; it wrapped her round when she rode downtown in their ancient Packard to heap scorn upon would-be developers. And it kept her from ever being easy with anyone, especially Jackie. Jackie, so easily moving into her happy marriage, setting up her potting studio, teaching, developing such a wide circle of friends. Their struggle, quiet as it was, had ended only in the older woman's death.

Yet in the hospital at the end, seeing that Jackie had flown back from a vacation in New Mexico, Little Granny reached out her hands, saying, "Thank God you came," as if reaching at last, before she slipped away, for what she had been missing in herself.

Driving home from the hospital that day, Jackie had felt a presence beside her in the car, Little Granny's presence. It was such a strong sensation that she had to stop and pull to the side of the road. The Bay glistened below at the foot of the hills, and San Francisco shimmered distantly. In those days the slope of the city's hills was not blocked by skyscrapers, and patches of green stood out among the frame houses, and the air was nearly always clear. A thought came to her: Now we can be friends. It was as if the thought had come from the dead woman, as if it were Little Granny's own thought. She wanted Jackie to know that death had released her from that tight puritanical knot and set her free. She was a presence there with Jackie, gentle, benign; they might have been enjoying the view together. Jackie felt uplifted, released. Now we can be friends. It was true.

Every year brought Jackie greater appreciation for the strength of the old woman who could let go only in death. For now she herself was the one who watched over the hill, who did her level best to ward off its destruction.

There had been times when she thought it would be pleasant to lead a simpler life, to travel more, to be free of property, of possessions. She was an artist herself and knew the artist's need of freedom that had inspired her father-in-law. But after all, her studio was here. The houses her husband's father had built were her tradition; she honored their beauty and grace. The important thing, she told herself, was not to fall into living *sparingly*, as so many older people seemed to do, but to enjoy the privileges she had: time to work in her studio and time to renovate her mind.

Up the hill behind the house, she and Mr. Wonderful walked into a grove of black acacias. They found two tall saplings. The young man brought out his tape measure again. The saplings were just the right length for the railing and about three inches in diameter, long and flexible. She raised the ax and in a short time made the sacrifices. She could still cut down a tree, tar a roof; she was very handy.

They brought the saplings down, cut off the side shoots, and rasped down the trunks until they were smooth. They lashed them to the posts and twined them with the saplings' own shoots. Then they oiled the limbs and posts with linseed oil.

She was satisfied with their work. When you grasped the railing coming up the walk, you grasped the round support of a tree. It looked as if it had always been there; it looked just right.

Alice Fong Yu

Born March 2, 1905

Alice Fong's washing machine, she says, was the south Yuba River near Marysville, where, as a child, she pounded clothes on the rocks. Raised in a family of six girls and five boys, she remembers the days before Chinese children were admitted in school. Her father ran a grocery for the Chinese people of the legendary gold mountain, worked the Omega mine, then, hoping for better conditions for his family, brought them to San Francisco in 1916.

Young Alice's successful fundraising for the Red Cross drew the attention of the director of that organization, who offered to help her enter San Francisco Normal Teacher's College, an unusual accomplishment for a Chinese woman of that time. She married a journalist, editor of a Chinese newspaper, and in the 1920s became the first Chinese teacher in San Francisco, at the Commodore Stockton Elementary School. The mother of two sons, she taught all her life until 1970.

She worked during World War II for the War Relief Association as a fundraiser. She is president of the Chinese Historical Society and the Chinese Culture Foundation. The recipient of many honors, including the Best Ten award from the San Francisco Examiner, she is also a frequently sought speaker.

RIGHT SPEECH

Early in the morning before the household stirred, she sat writing at the table below the shelves that held all her Chinese ornaments and mementos, gifts from all her friends who had gone to visit China—an ivory fan, little enameled boxes, painted eggs. She scribbled some notes: develop a loving and caring nature; be kind, helpful, considerate, compassionate, conscientious, and more human versus denial of life and liberty to others. She wanted to work all that in somehow.

"Ma, are you writing another speech?" It was Alon, shrugging on his silk jacket. He always set an example for his employees at the restaurant and looked impeccable when he left for work. "You must learn to say no. Two letters: *n–o*. You can do it; I know you can."

"Well, it's Chinese New Year; they thought of me as a speaker."

He shook his head. "You'll get sick if you keep this up. You're retired now, remember?"

And busier than she'd ever been. Alon liked things the old way: keep the ancient Chinese woman at home, if only to honor her the more. The new way was a bit more tiring: stand her up to make a speech whenever there was a need for some reminders of tradition, of the natural harvest of wisdom that is supposed to accrue with years.

"Next time, *n–o*. I know you can do it, Ma."

"I'm making SS if you want to have lunch later," she said. They played a little initials game, she and Alon. SS stood for Soup Stock. She was a PP, Pokey Person, with an MM, Memorabilia Museum, the shelves filled with her Chinese mementos.

"Don't try to change the subject, Ma," he said, giving her a kiss. And he was off to the restaurant, where he kept his no's in perfect balance. No to the cook who was too slow, no to the bok choy supplier if the greens came withered, no to the overflow customers who wanted to be seated immediately.

Alice had heard a lot of no's all of her life; no wonder she didn't like to say them. Long ago she realized she was different when the neighborhood children chanted, "Sing-song-China-man," cringing away from her, unwilling even to touch a Chinese child in the circle games during recess. Barbarians, she learned to call them, a word she had learned early, as soon as she learned of her Chinese heritage. She decided to study to teach in China, even though she was a third-generation American. To prepare she went to San Francisco Normal Teacher's College, as it was called then, and a gentleman named Frederick Burke tried to turn her away. "You wouldn't be hired for a job anywhere in this country," he told her. But she had her indignant reply ready, flew off the handle, in fact. She wouldn't teach here if they begged her; she was going to China to help her own people. He let her register.

She didn't go to China. Somewhere along the line the no's became only a murmur. Her sons were glad. "We're Americans, Mom. China would have been a big mistake." She never got to see the place her grandparents had come from. Of course, they had brought the traditions with them. Because he had daughters, her grandfather had decided one of the girls had to have the status of the "golden lily" so that she might get a good husband, and there in that little California mining town her mother's feet had been bound. Her father, working his gold mountain, had found her mother, bound feet and all.

Alice got her degree, married, and started teaching. The principal of the school where she'd done her practice teaching couldn't do without her. She had been so relieved to have someone who understood the school's students, who were all Chinese, that she told the college she'd hire Alice as soon as she got her credential. She was the first Chinese-American teacher in San Francisco. Thousands of her people had learned their lessons through her.

She looked at the speech she was writing. Right speech. At fifty-seven she had decided to get another degree, in speech therapy. There were so many people who needed help, whose speech wasn't just right. When her other son, Joal, had needed help with his speech, she learned that she had a knack for helping with the right placement of the tongue. So she had started on a wonderful new career: working with children, young people who were stuck, getting their tongues and lips to move into the right groove. The work brought a lot of laughter with it, and love. One little girl couldn't say "lady." Alice taught her all the labials, starting with love, love, love, so that "wady" eventually became "lady." Long after her therapy was over, the girl would poke her head into the office to say "hello," not "hewoe"; she had gotten it right forever. And there was that antagonistic football star who didn't want to take the time. He was the epitome of strength; how could anything be wrong with him? She decided to show him how it looked, his side *s*, all those *s*'s coming only from the side of his mouth—sa-se-si-so-su, she demonstrated for him. That did it. He eased his magnificent body down into the chair. He had to *take* the time he realized.

It was her innovation to take ten students at a time who had the same problem and teach them together—kindergarten through sixth grade. That became the most logical method. That became the standard way of doing it. It makes the children feel better too—not singled out, not awful, not victims of no's, just kids with something they need to learn, *can* learn.

She wrote another line or two on her New Year's speech. She wanted her advice to make sense; if only later, when the young people were older, they might remember it. She scribbled something else; she wanted to be sure to say that one must eat only 80 percent of capacity. For health.

She'd probably never do as Alon wished. Next time she'd tell him she forgot to say no and tease him a bit with their private code. A Pokey Person always forgets, she might say.

Maybe she would add an NN code to their little game, No No's.

Louise M. Davies

Born May 23, 1900

The woman who gave the San Francisco Symphony its hall doesn't like the term philanthropy, a word she feels has unflattering connotations. She prefers volunteer or being able to give. Whichever name she gives it, she has influenced many other volunteer contributors and has a fulltime job at the awesome task of giving away her own money.

Born in gold country, in Quincy, California, into a middle-class ranch family, she says, "I turned out by fortune." She believes her early years on her family's ranch were a nourishing foundation for a good life. The family moved to Oakland, where her mother decided to end her marriage. She took her children to Bellevue, near Seattle, Washington, and took in boarders. Later Louise went to a convent school in Oakland, where she became a Catholic convert. In her early twenties she met Ralph Davies, who had what we now call an entry-level job at Standard Oil. They were married in 1925.

Within ten years after their marriage, Ralph Davies was doing well enough that they were able to buy twelve acres in Woodside, and a few years later they built the house where Louise still lives today. During World War II, while she was serving as a nurse's aide, Ralph Davies was appointed Deputy Petroleum Administrator for War, service for which President Truman later gave him the Award of Merit. After the war, he formed the American Independent Oil Company and acquired the Natomas Company and the American President Lines. Before he died in 1971, Ralph Davies had earned a fortune that has become almost a public trust because of his many endowments. Only one bears his name, the Ralph K. Davies Medical Center, and it was named after his death.

Louise's guideline for endowing funds, she says, came from her husband: Limit yourself to what really interests you, just a few things. She decided upon music and education. She has made gifts to Stanford University, the University of San Francisco, and many parochial schools, as well as her more widely publicized gift of Symphony Hall.

She has three daughters and five grandchildren. One of her granddaughters, Lucy Lewis, a playwright in her twenties, has a special bond with her grandmother and is a frequent visitor to the Woodside house.

VOLUNTEER

Dites moi pourquoi la vie est belle,
Dites moi pourquoi la vie est gai…

Lucy says, "We'll be finishing dinner, and Nana will say, 'Well, it's time for a song. Lucy, let's hear "Born Free." Or how about "Raindrops Are Falling on My Head"?'"

Louise Davies has catholic taste in music, though at the symphony she prefers the classics, Mozart and Bach. "She always made us stand up and sing at the table," says Lucy. "Everyone sings around Nana. We used to sing all the way to church. Just now we were singing a Noel Coward song, 'I'll See You Again,' because a friend is here whose mother has died. You just want to cry."

Louise enjoys all five of her grandchildren. She says, "There's no tension between us; it's a generation thing. My daughter Ellen paints beautifully. I said, 'Ellen, why don't you go back to painting?' She said, 'Well, Mother, I will'; as if to say, it's not your business. Your own children don't want you to tell them what to do, but with grandchildren it's a little freer.

"Look, my three daughters are so different from me because, in the first place, everything was given to them. I walked five miles to school, but for my daughters we had a bus, or I took them. I think it does something for your morale if you have to struggle as a child to get to school five miles away, even if you go on horseback."

Remembering her early years in Quincy, she says, "I think that many people who have made a dent in the world, even a small dent, have come from small towns, and this is because they have to think independently. In fact, the first suffragette in the whole United States came from right up near Quincy."

When her mother left her father and moved to Bellevue, Washington, she took in roomers in a big country place. "We had cows; she milked them, and we delivered the milk. We had a lot of chickens. I used to peddle eggs and milk in Bellevue.

"I used to blame my mother for the breakup of my parents' marriage because my father had very likable qualities. He also had a terrible temper. But my mother would never retreat. I couldn't have been my mother because she would fight back. Oh, I must say, I wasn't a pussycat though.

"My mother was lovely. I think that all the kindness I have comes from my mother. She had a big soul, shall I say? She used to go out to what we called the poorhouse in Oakland once or twice a week, and she sewed for those people out there. She was always helping somebody."

Louise was twelve, in an Oakland convent school, when she became a Catholic convert. "I don't know why my mother put me in the convent. Maybe she thought it was a good idea, and in a way it was the best thing she ever did for me. I got a wonderful education and I 'got religion,' as they say. It has guided my life; it gave me direction. The nuns were so dedicated and so happy, contented. It made them strong women, really powerful women. You don't see much of that. Most people lead sort of fractured lives. I do myself. Yet I seem to have a kind of drive."

That drive was directed toward becoming an actress when she was in her teens. "Oh, I was going to be the greatest actress in the world. In the convent school we used to put on plays, Greek plays. I was always the lead, because I wanted to be, I guess! I went to work when I was eighteen, and I was in a lot of plays then, in Oakland. I really thought I was pretty good. I liked acting. But then I decided I would rather be married and have children."

It was during a visit to a resort on the Russian River that she met Ralph Davies, who was then in the very early stages of living out the American dream of becoming a self-made millionaire. Later he visited her in Los Angeles, where she had a stenographic job. Deciding that her heart was in San Francisco, she moved back to Oakland and took a job in San Francisco. Ralph was working for Standard Oil; he had started as an office boy for the company when he was fourteen. They rode the ferry home together, "where the seagulls followed us all the way to Oakland." His proposal came after a walk around Lake Merritt. "He pulled a hairpin out of my hair and twisted it around my ring finger. 'Does it fit?' he asked. I had been waiting six months for that to happen."

They were married in 1925, and after their honeymoon, they moved into a one-bedroom cottage in Ross, where Louise's education in money management began. "For some reason I thought he made a large salary, so I blithely wrote checks all over nearby San Anselmo for kitchenwares, furniture, and appliances. Every check bounced! Ralph was forced to tell me that he earned only $350 a month. Near the end of our second year Ralph decided to put me on an allowance.

"We had no car, no telephone at first, and we tried to be vegetarians. We were idealists. We were going to be open with each other, tell all our thoughts, emotions, and feelings—and we did try. However, it soon became apparent we had quite different reactions to things and we had better stick to what we could agree on. They ought to have schools for wives, and schools for taking care of people."

In her later years Ralph's mother came to live with them. "She was darling, sweet, and awfully old, I thought. Seventy. A very 'visity' old lady. It didn't matter if the beds weren't made; she'd say 'Well now, let's have a nice visit.' We didn't have people like that in my family. It was first get the work done, then sit down. I'm still like that. If I want to write a letter, I have to go and do my other chores first. It's a habit. She loved to sit and tell stories. She'd tell you about her dreams. She always thought dreams meant something. She'd swirl the tea leaves around in the cup, and she'd say, 'This is what's going to happen.'"

During those years, Louise yielded to her mother-in-law's desire to have breakfast alone with Ralph. "I would stay in bed or out of the way in the morning so she could have Ralph to herself. This was something that was very difficult for me, but I knew it was good for her, and it made her happy to do it. And he wanted that little period without me. After all, they'd lived together until he was twenty-eight. But I felt sorry that I wasn't really a companion to her. I could not enter her world."

Even though they shared the same religion, there was a difference. Her mother-in-law had a rosary but went to church only for weddings or funerals or holidays. "Entirely different from me. I became a Catholic because I wanted to, and I wouldn't know what to do with life if I hadn't become one."

She has, of course, found plenty to do with her life and its wealth. Volunteering, perhaps inspired by her mother's example, has become her way of life, most notably with her involvement with the symphony and the hall. "I guess I am self-motivated. I went to them about giving the hall; they didn't come to me. Other people—a lot of people—would do it if they knew how and would enjoy giving. Some people don't seem to enjoy having their money. It was a great pleasure for me to give that, and it would be for anybody, because you see people enjoying the hall."

She has given money both to universities and to elementary schools. "I want to go into the poor parochial schools to give fellowships to Hispanics and blacks. One of my daughters, Maryon, Lucy's mother, is working to try to up the salaries and to make schools more effective."

Her Catholicism, however, is not entirely parochial. "I went to a retreat recently, and the priest was really quite deep. He gave me a book, *The Future of Man* by Teilhard de Chardin, in which he claims we're evolving, getting smarter. All those genes that come together to make up a person, those genes really are from everywhere. It's almost a proof of how we're all related spiritually. I'm sure the time will come when all Christian religions recognize the same source."

Perhaps such views enable her to feel relaxed about granddaughter Lucy's plays, which are somewhat anticlerical. One of them, set in a convent school, was produced by the Magic Theater.

"The kid who is put into a parochial school is often a victim," Lucy said, "caught between parent and school. I was afraid that Nana would object to this play. In the past she has ignored things I've written that are critical of the church, but this one is pretty blatant."

Apparently the production had no impact on the strong bond of affection between them. Lucy reminisced about a visit her grandmother made when she was in school in Georgetown. "I was doing a special seminar in an honors class for which we were reading *Robinson Crusoe*. Nana came to a tea party where everybody was talking about the deep meaning of the book. One man said he was a Christ figure, and somebody said it was a novel of adventure, and everybody was being very articulate and intellectual, showing off, juxtaposing various ideas. And suddenly Nana says, 'Whoa, I've got to get a plane. Lucy, get me a taxi.' And as we were leaving, she stunned everybody by coming out with, '*Robinson Crusoe*—I always thought it was about the birth of a soul.' Not a bad exit line.

"Nana keeps trying to give me a quilt she bought from the Amish when she visited me at the University of Iowa. She keeps trying to give us her jewelry. We say, 'No, Nana, we don't want to think about your jewelry.' She says, 'What's wrong, don't you like it?' I'm always explaining to Nana that I don't want *things*."

Despite the wish to distribute her jewelry among family members, Lucy says the impulse isn't out of a sense that she may not have use for it herself. "Nana has no idea she is old. She loses her friends—someone will die, and she feels sad about it—but doesn't think it could be happening to her."

Asked if their relationship is close, Lucy says, "Yes, she drives me crazy! Right now we're having a big fight. I've come down to Woodside to try to persuade her to get a driver. She has attacks of vertigo. A friend of mine wanted to talk to her about some money for Hispanic students, and Nana called up and couldn't do it because of vertigo. I thought, what if she had an attack in the car? So I have to get her to find somebody she can phone to drive her. She might throw me out of the house. I've gotten thrown out so many times about various things, not going to church and so on. She'll say, 'Never come back.' Then she'll phone me and say, 'Oh, Lucy, you're coming down, aren't you? So-and-so's going to be here—we'll have a picnic.'"

There would be singing at any picnic. Louise spoke of a group of nuns she has become especially fond of, the sisters at St. Patrick's Seminary. "Those are the nuns who cook for the boys who are going to become priests. They're French, from Quebec. I've known them forever. A long time ago they were cloistered: they couldn't go out. Once up at my house in Tahoe, Father Munier said, 'You know, those little nuns can't go anyplace. Why don't you go down and see them, and if you care to you could invite them up here. That would be all right with me.' So it started a long time ago. I would invite them up here, and we would have tea and sing in French, all kinds of songs, just for ourselves. And they came at Christmas too. The last time, I had neighborhood children come, and they sang for them. It's kind of nice. They don't see children; all they see are those young men at the seminary. So the neighborhood children came in and sang and talked to them, and helped."

Margaret Murdock

Born June 22, 1894   Died June 10, 1985

For nearly six decades the bells in the Campanile at the University of California, Berkeley campus, were rung by a delicate, slender woman whose bright red hair slowly turned silvery white as she became what she calls "part of the public domain." In 1918 Margaret Murdock received a master's degree in education on that campus, and throughout her working life and some years beyond, she remained a part of it.

A native San Franciscan, with family roots in Oroville, California, Margaret took her first job in the office of the dean of women; then she worked in the president's office, then as a credentials counselor in the education department. Her avocation as musician in the Campanile started in 1923.

She drew the attention of Charles Kurault, who showed her at work on his television segment, "On the Road." She accompanied Garff Wilson's recording of Dickens's Christmas Carol *on the bells.*

Her housemate for several decades was design professor Hope Gladding, who shared her philosophy that older people should not live alone, but should seek ways to be mutually supportive. Margaret continued as volunteer bell-ringer after her retirement, until she was 87.

RINGING CHANGES

For the six o'clock concert nobody else was about. The janitor was gone, and the elevator man as well. Only a few students were passing by from the library. She let herself into the building, unlocked the elevator door, and glided up. Then she took the thirty-nine steps. Margaret always joked about it—thirty-nine steps to the tower. It was lovely up there alone in the Campanile at dusk, with the sunset glow slanting through the tower windows onto the bell wires.

There was a slight breeze coming in from the Bay, as always at this hour; today it was sharper than usual. The air was clear; she could see the bridge, the traffic on the water. It seemed as if it was only the other day that you had to ride the ferry boat to this side of the Bay; yet everyone took the bridge for granted now. She herself drove across it twice a week to work for the historical society.

She let herself into the glass cubicle, sat before the immense keyboard, and reached up to adjust the wires. They were always sensitive to temperature changes, especially these new ones. They would be expanded now with the warmth of the westering sun.

Ten minutes to go. She rubbed the cushions of her hands to get them ready to hammer the large wooden keys. How much easier the action had been when there were only twelve chimes. But thirty-six had been added by an alumna contribution. During many weeks she had gone below into the practice room, had come early to try to do her duty by the new bells, all fifty plus. But she knew the four chromatic octaves had turned her into a fossil. And now there was talk of accepting another contribution: thirteen more bells. She shook her head. Not today. Today was for appreciation.

Margaret was twenty-nine when she started playing the chimes. It was a campus project then. You didn't have to be a musician. The first chimesmaster was head of the German department. He had liked assigning hymns for her program (in those days they played mostly hymns on the chimes), always choosing hymns by some composer named Redhead, because of her own red hair. His idea of a joke.

Then a music teacher who didn't have enough pupils was put in charge of the tower, and he didn't even want his students to know he was a bellringer, in such low esteem was the occupation held. And after that two men in the accounting department took over. But throughout, she'd been a ringer, even after her retirement, even after Hope, her housemate of forty years, had gone into the retirement home and sold the house, and she had gone to live at the Faculty Club; still she'd volunteered to go on ringing. She would chase over to play mornings, or whenever she was needed. She'd been a bellringer longer than anyone else.

And now it was all to become part of the music department. People would make a career of it, go to train in Belgium.

She looked through the music she'd brought and placed it up on the rack. "Hanging Danny Deever" today, because exams were starting tomorrow. The mournful tolling always amused her, but she doubted many of the students nowadays remembered the tradition. Many of them appreciated the bells though. Sometimes they even came up to the tower to thank her.

The most responsive audience she had ever had at the tower was the group of hand bellringers, high school kids mostly; knowing they played Bach's "Bourée" she was able to show them how it sounded on the tower bells. She'd even joined a handbell group herself, where hymns were rung as well as folk music. She loved the round clarity of their sound in churches, loved the fun among the ringers, for they were either adolescents or oldsters like herself—it was good for the generations to find a meeting ground in bells.

Folk music always found a place on her program. Once during World War II, a patriot complained about her playing an Italian folk song. She had been called into the president's office: "There's a report, Margaret, that you're playing Fascist songs on the chimes." A folk song!

There had been other complaints, especially from the math department. The letter in the campus newspaper from the math professor: "The bells are a pest, a form of tyranny. We are compelled either to listen or to leave town." And the other mathematics professor who objected to tunes, who wanted only "change" music. She could ring changes, the mathematical sequence Dorothy Sayers made the center of her mystery *The Nine Tailors.* She had taught it to herself using the *Encyclopaedia Britannica.* Sometimes she'd ring them when she was sure one of the math professors was around, ringing the sequences, from bell to bell, never repeating herself, one times two times three and so on. With twelve bells she could keep on for several hours and have more than a thousand changes before getting back to the first sequence. Quite a little game.

Weren't the mathematicians too inflexible? After all, why not learn the meaning of the word *change,* see its connection to life? You had to go with what was coming next, even if it was tunes on the chimes or a whole enormous carillon of bells. You had to allow things to move along, or give up your nostalgia. Nothing remained the same, not even the ringing of changes.

Lately, giving things away had been her way of accepting change. She had sent all the books from her father's press, Blair-Murdock Company, to the Bancroft Library's special collection. All the personal treasures she had let go of in order to accept change, to enjoy it. She would enjoy being at her sister's on the walnut ranch, with the view of Mount Lassen from her bedroom window. She had good memories of the campus, six decades of them; she wouldn't count her losses.

She flexed her wrists and reached out for the keys. The bells, crisp and brilliant, rang out. She remembered how the opening sounds always surprised tower visitors, who looked in at her, pressing their hands over their ears; excited by the sounds, they lingered. Students, especially, found the bells gave them an unexpected high. How exhilarated they were whenever she took the elevator down with them! Often up there by herself, as she played, she sang at the top of her voice.

In just a few moments now she would take the elevator down for the last time, glide away unnoticed. She had arranged it so that no one would notice her going. If you can go out without being noticed and still do something worthwhile, that is happiness.

She finished the final phrase of "Danny Deever" and started to sing the notes of her last melody, "Farewell to Thee."

Jane Hollister Wheelwright

Born September 9, 1905

Jane Hollister and her twin brother, Clinton, were born in Sacramento, California, but shortly thereafter were taken by their parents to live for a time in Mexico. Jane learned to speak Spanish before she spoke English. When she was three, the family moved to the ranch near Santa Barbara, a family legacy, which her father managed.

After being sent away to boarding school and college, her Uncle Lincoln Steffens rescued her, as she puts it, by inviting her to live with his family, first in Italy, then in England, where she was exposed to some of the most exciting minds of the day. In 1929 she married Joseph Wheelwright, and they traveled extensively; their first child, Lynda, was born in China.

In Zurich they met C.G. Jung, and that was a turning point in their lives.

Jung advised her husband to get a medical degree, so they lived in London while Joe studied medicine. Their son, John, was born there in 1934. In the late thirties they returned to Zurich to work with Jung and completed their study of analytical psychology before World War II began.

They returned to San Francisco and started a practice, and with Elizabeth Whitney and Lucille Elliott (also in this volume) cofounded what is now called the C.G. Jung Institute of San Francisco. In the 1960s Jane started to work with patients who were terminally ill, which led to the writing of her book The Death of a Woman.

In recent years, Jane and her daughter, Lynda, have begun to work closely together, and she told us the story of a workshop.

CHANGING WOMAN

One of the workshop participants stood up to challenge Jane for her use of the word *passé*. Jane turned to Lynda—had she really called herself passé? Lynda's blue eyes lighted up in amusement. Then everybody was talking at once, not a rare thing in this enthusiastic group.

They had received her paper well, "The Power of the Maiden." They understood her: let the maiden archetype in ourselves give us access to all female experience, that of both future and past as felt through daughter, wife, mother, worker, wise woman. The Navajos had always known of these capacities, acknowledged them in their "changing-woman goddess," while our modern world stumbled along with two roles, "young girl" and "old girl." Wasn't it the maiden in a woman's psyche, for example, who prompted a woman with children to go back to college or to take a plunge into some new adventure?

The woman who had raised the question prevailed. "You can't be passé if you're both wise old woman and daughter, say, at the same time."

The word certainly did sound off key, out-of-date, a slip perhaps because she'd been so aware of the difference between her style and Lynda's. She was marvelous, her daughter, now in her fifties, and, as always, funny, incisive, candid, quick-witted as she gave her talk about their strained relationship, with its origins in her early childhood. That was doubtless why she felt a little out of it, yet passé; her own paper was waiting to be read. She couldn't talk in a lively, off-the-cuff manner as Lynda did and still be sure of covering all of her controversial ideas.

Her husband, Joe, spoke over the murmur of the other voices. One of the four men in the workshop—there were fifty women—Joe had been unusually restrained, deferring to her and Lynda, as indeed he believed he must even when it wasn't their occasion, yet so biologically dominant with that voice he could throw a mile, his lean towering height, his exuberance. "Jane has just shot out like Halley's comet these last few years," he was saying over everybody, "leaves me sitting contentedly in the corner, a husband with his knitting."

Really, she had to stop him. "It's not that I've shot out," Jane said. "I've been an observer for a long time."

"Shy," Joe suggested.

"No," and she felt very firm about it. "I just didn't think I was ready to say anything."

Smiling, Joe glanced down at his hands—they held something he was rubbing with his handkerchief. A little Chinese bell someone had placed on the table to call people in for the sessions.

Another hand waved. "How did you—get ready?"

An image rose before her of the ranch, with the Santa Ynez Mountains above her childhood home. On their last visit to their own house on the ridge, a mountain lion had strolled out of the chaparral to sit quietly in a small clearing and gaze up at the house in a leisurely fashion, like an omen, the impossible becoming possible. Eventually it calmly strolled back into the brush-covered boulders.

In that wilderness of 40,000 acres, she and her twin brother, Clinty, had raised themselves. Their mother, with her doctorate signed by Kaiser Wilhelm, passed her days with books and occasional adult visitors. Children were not allowed inside except for meals. And so Jane and her brother had roamed the mountains, hiked the vast sweep of grazing land that went all the way down to the sea, and grew up talking Rattlesnake and Cow and Red-tailed Hawk, as Joe put it. Of course, Mother had believed in education and had sent her east to Bryn Mawr, but the lessons of the wilderness had taken hold. College felt superficial and pointless; she left after her freshman year. The ranch had taught her self-sufficiency and that life should be adventure, and when Joe came into her life, they decided to see the world together. They were married, then started out, steerage class. Two years later, in China, Lynda's birth brought them in touch with the normal consequence of marriage. Like her mother before her, Jane had no calling for the conventional art of nurture. Lynda and John, when he came along, inherited the legacy of ranch life, with all its mixed blessings.

Only long after she and Joe had begun to study with Jung did she realize how she had repeated her mother's pattern: she had asked the ranch to serve as mother to her children as well. Daily contact with the earth had yielded its cthonic wisdom, but the civilized mind demands its own development even though it may be rooted in the primitive. She felt a need to bring these divisions together.

In the meantime the lives of her children unfolded, often on the ranch with their grandparents. After Jane and Joe had set up their practice, a suppressed desire grew in Lynda to be a patient, the favored being, Lynda later said. She became attached to the idea of her elegant, learned father—idea because, of course, Joe, preoccupied with his profession, was more absent even than Jane. Lynda joined the ranks of what she now calls "father's daughters," the subject of her talk at the workshop. She worked passionately, became a high achiever; she studied anthropology, then switched to psychology, became adept at linearity of thought, and ended up with a master's degree in social work. Yet, like Jane, she never lost touch with her instincts; the ranch had made its mark.

Jane returned to the question: How do you get ready? "I go back to the ranch," she said. "It's there I prepare everything I write." The ranch always told her when she was ready to say something. Both she and Lynda had come to realize that they had the same mother and that it was the ranch.

Lynda said, "And, then, not long ago, my mother wrote a book."

The book was about Sally, her young patient dying of cancer. After learning that her disease would kill her, Sally fell into a severe depression, and an analyst friend persuaded her to let Jane come to work with her at her home. Jane had to cut through to Sally's unfinished business, foregoing the leisurely realizations of conventional analysis, to help this frail, often-despairing woman find meaning in her life and acceptance of the illuminations that may come at the approach of death.

Sally's dreams poured out immediately, conveying to her the great potential for development available to her. She summoned amazing courage. Her spirit began to unfold, and her dreams guided her to immeasurable growth in a very short while.

As she worked with Sally, Jane's concern deepened beyond that for the usual patient. She found herself thinking often of the mother-daughter dilemma, so dramatically presented in Sally's dreams. Lynda was close to Sally's age. Perhaps that had something to do with her decision to write Sally's story; Jane thought it could hearten and encourage others, yet there was more to it than that. Analysis is always a two-way process. As Jane worked on the book *The Death of a Woman*, Lynda could have been, unknowingly, Sally.

Writing was hard for her. She realized she was clumsy with phrases. She was a stickler for accuracy, which kept her on course but cluttered up her style. After all, she was a college dropout, even if she was an analyst.

A clear message came to her in a dream, in which she asked Lynda to edit a paper of hers, and Lynda agreed to do it. "Because it is a dream," Lynda said within the dream. When Jane awoke, she decided to act upon her dream, and Lynda agreed to help her. Their strong connection began to surface. Appropriately, it hinged on Lynda's free style and Jane's ideas.

As they got into the work and Lynda read Jane's book, a slow understanding came to them both. "I like what you write," Lynda told her, "because it shows you to me as I've never seen you before." *As a mother*, Jane realized. In treating Sally, she had called upon her strongest nurturing power: total acceptance.

Sally's story brought Lynda's own nurturing power into play. As they worked on other papers about women, the process became a sowing for them of the nourishment they both had missed in their lives, each providing it for the other.

Lynda said, "You know what we should do? We should go back to the ranch, take a long hike together. Go home."

It was there, high in the mountains above the sea, that the idea of this workshop came to fruition for the two of them. They felt no end in sight for their mutual enrichment.

"It's a gift," Lynda said. An unexpected gift. They could only thank the years of work on themselves that had brought it about.

"But how can *I* do it?" a woman only slightly younger than Jane wanted to know.

Jane said, "I'll tell you part of a recent dream of mine. I am looking for a place to sit in tightly packed pews in a rectangular area where a spontaneous divine revelation is about to happen. Popelike figures are standing nearby as witnesses. I come to a young woman in a dark shawl. She gives off a religious feeling, and there is an ageless youthfulness about her. She is participating in the mystery. She signals me to sit next to her. The message to me is that *she* takes the initiative. She, as a young woman, is as important as I, the old woman, in this religious scene." And both, of course, were Jane herself.

The woman nodded, understanding.

Jean Christie Lien

Born June 29, 1891   Died February 13, 1984

"I had an enchanted childhood," Jean Lien said. She was born in Turkey during the massacre by the Turks of the Armenians to American parents who defended the Armenian cause. Her father was the president of a Presbyterian college for boys, St. Paul's College; and in the compound of the school and the Christie home, thousands of Armenians found sanctuary and eventual passage to the United States. Jean grew up speaking English, French, and Turkish. She returned to the United States to study and was graduated from Wellesley in the class of 1915 and earned a master's degree in philosophy from Columbia University in 1916. She returned abroad to direct a YMCA in France the following year and remained there throughout World War I.

Some years later she came home to a teaching job at Occidental College in California, where she met Eugene Lien, a student in her French class. They were married in 1935. They later moved to Berkeley, where Eugene was working on a doctorate at the outbreak of World War II. When he returned from the war, he studied further and began to teach, eventually becoming head of mathematics in the Oakland school system.

Childless, Jean began to work as a babysitter in 1944, when a neighbor needed help with her child. Many other children followed, all of whom remained lifelong friends.

The childhood that had given her the foundation of a happy life returned to her often, brilliant visual far memories.

FAR MEMORY

A little girl walks along the path toward the barn with a stork just her own height. They stroll in a companionable way, the stork's huge webbed feet splaying out. The little girl, dressed in a white pinafore, speaks playfully to the bird, for they are good friends. "Snowball," the little girl says…

If only she could hear more, but they vanish, and Jean opens her eyes to look out her window at the Lombardy poplars twinkling in the sun. Sometimes a memory such as that of the stork with the sun glinting on its downy wings at her side would arise with her eyes open. The person or the creature would appear, vivid, colorful, with the same magic as in her childhood. How well she remembered it all!

Did she have a picture of the stork? That was its name, Snowball. She called to Eugene to bring her the album from her childhood. He fetched it for her, saying he was happy to have her home and hoped she mended soon.

She told him what she had said to Dr. Coen. "I said the evil eye got me. Remember, just before my ninetieth birthday I boasted that I had gone all my ninety years without breaking a single bone? I told him what the old Greek woman said to me when I was a little girl, that you have to spit over your left shoulder if you brag. The evil eye is so vigilant that it saw I forgot to spit." She smiled. "For a while there Dr. Coen didn't realize I was joking." She had fallen the week before and fractured a vertebra. There was nothing she could do for a time now except lie perfectly still.

Somehow, as she lay here, everything from her childhood was coming back in beautiful, drifting images. Eugene fetched the little album she had brought from Europe, and they both looked at it. On its very last page was a picture of their wedding. They would save that for last, and she would savor the memory of how young he had looked. They didn't have a formal wedding. They'd just rushed off together, and when they got back, they dressed in their best and went to a photographer. Eugene was only twenty-six and she was forty-three. She had joked about that to him, "I won't have to worry about being left a widow." Lately he seemed to be catching up with her.

There was the photograph of Snowball, just as she had remembered. She said, "The boys used to take the stork down to the lake, and Mother would give us a cake of Ivory soap, shipped all the way from Boston, and we would wash him." She turned a page. "And here is the mulberry tree. Did I ever tell you of my love affair with that tree?"

"No," Eugene lied, and she knew he was lying. He loved to hear about her tree and how she used to talk to it, thinking it quite exceptional because it had grown to such enormous size. She would put her arms about it and climb up into its great protective branches. One stormy night, in a state of terrible fear, she had run to her tree to offer it protection, for she thought that the storm would hurt it, that lightning might strike it, and she wanted to defend it from the storm. Of course, her mother never understood, but Jean loved to be afraid, enjoyed the fearful storm, the wind beating on her skin, and the rain. From the tree she had looked out on the village with the factory across the street, knowing that in spite of her fear she and her tree were safe as long as they were together.

She closed her eyes and in a moment heard Eugene in another part of the house.

The camel bell sounds, so she leaps from bed and jumps into her clothes, knowing it is Tuesday and the woodsman is coming through the big stone gate with the load of wood he always stacks beside the hedge. "Did you bring me something?" she asks him. His face betrays he has forgotten the usual piece of candy or fruit, so he lifts her up in his huge arms and sets her upon the camel, between its humps, and guides the camel about the yard, careful to avoid the tree branches. "Don't get knocked off," the woodsman says.

Eugene set a tray with some lemonade on her bedside table. "Are you thirsty?" She smiled a thank you.

"People were always bringing me things when I was small," she told him. "A quail once, a fox. And then there was Monsieur Ibou."

The camel driver reaches into the bosom of his jacket and comes forth with something hidden in both palms of his hands. She peers inside and sees it is a baby owl. "I found it in the mountains, alone and hurt," the woodsman says. She takes the owl to the nice dark basement and brings food to him every day. When the owl hears her crossing the floor above him, he hoots out to her, whoo-whoo. After he has eaten, she reads to him, knowing he is a very wise creature and would probably enjoy a story. She chooses the Bible for him, story after story.

M. Ibou grows to an enormous size. People called him an eagle owl.

Father and Mother are telling her that she must go away to boarding school. She says, "But, Mother, I can't leave my owl." Mother and Father confer about this problem.

And now M. Ibou sits next to her on the train. The conductor, a friend from the village whom everybody calls "Six-Toe-Man," asks if M. Ibou is comfortable; and, of course, he is. "I myself am a little thirsty," she says. After a while, the train begins to slow down; she looks around for Six-Toe-Man to ask him why the train is stopping—they aren't near a town. And then, outside the window, she sees him, sauntering into a field where there is a well, and he brings a drink up to her window. So fresh and cool from his dipper.

What a gift these memories were! She was so grateful for them. She had always hoped one day to write these stories, to make them into a book for children. She had enjoyed telling them when she was sitting for the children here in the neighborhood. Eugene would have liked that too, she knew, a little book. He had planted a redwood tree up the hillside for every child she had taken care of, more than fifty trees. Such a large family they had!

Eugene said, "Have your lemonade." He always knew when she was thirsty. "And then you might like to look at these, since you're thinking of the past." He had brought a packet of letters that she had written so many years ago.

"Is something the matter?" He seemed so worried. She didn't like to worry him. She wanted to make him easy about things. He took such good care of her, had ever since that first day he came to her class, walked her home, and never left. Impossible, a thing not done in those days. She said, "I love this part of my life as much as the beginning, you know. These are the 'yes' years, when there is so much we can do—see our friends, write letters, read old ones. I might even make a book of stories for the children." He returned her smile but sat a little heavily in the chair.

An unrelieved expanse of snow, vast, fearful. Henri Imer has brought her and some of the other girls from the pension into the Swiss mountains. They are lost, utterly lost. Henri says, "In union there is strength," so together they are shouting. Such a faint little chorus they make, and Jean, so tired, sinks down into the snow. She can hear her heart pounding against its white unknown depth. She is so tired, so sleepy. Henri, shaking her, seems very worried, then he, too, looks as sleepy as she. Light opens around her as she grows drowsier, a mysterious light. But then there is a beautiful sound of woofing. She lifts her head, and dogs as large as tigers come prancing over the snow. One of them nudges her, gently nibbles at her wrist. Henri says, "He wants you to pull the string that unties his blanket. She brushes the snow off his blanket, and he nudges her again. Tied under his chin is a little barrel, and Henri lets her drink its contents. She feels a strong sting from the liquid and thinks she has never tasted anything so delicious. Then there are monks, who have followed the footprints of the dogs. "Thank heaven you called out," the monks say. "You might have died overnight." The monks guide them up the mountainside to the monastery.

"I came home from that trip with such a flowing love of dogs," she murmured. Eugene was gazing out the window. *"You might have died overnight,"* the monk had said.

She opened the packet of letters Eugene had brought her. These were the love letters that she wrote to him before they were married, written about such interesting things. Look, there were abbreviations in them, a code they had devised perhaps—she couldn't remember what they meant. Perhaps Eugene would remember, but she didn't want to ask him, not just now, he looked so downcast.

She opened the album to that last picture, the one taken on their wedding day, his tender young face so inexperienced. How confident he was that their love would last though. He had been so determined to marry her, even though she was so many years his senior. *"I won't have to worry about being left a widow."* The thought, so flippant when she spoke it years ago, completed itself as she looked at her husband, understanding his heaviness now, the grief that was not very far away for him.

Lucille Elliott

Born July 11, 1893

Lucille Elliott expressed gratitude that the suffragettes "had won the battle" before she began to study medicine. A quarter of her class, starting in 1919 at University of California Medical Center, were women, and she said at that time there was considerable deference to the talented female doctor. Born in Arizona, Lucille grew up on a farm with her older sister and two brothers. She received her medical degree in 1924 and practiced medicine for most of her career.

In the late twenties she entered Jungian analysis with Elizabeth Whitney and later decided to study with Jung in Zurich. When she returned to this country, she divided her practice between analysis and medicine for some years,

then later devoted herself wholly to analysis. In 1943, with Whitney and Jane and Joseph Wheelwright, she founded what became the C.G. Jung Institute of San Francisco and was its president in 1948. She continued to practice and give courses to candidates of the institute's training program until her retirement in the seventies. She was an active member of the Congregational church, which she felt was a personal support in her work and philosophy.

The decision to enter a nursing home cannot be an easy one, but she spoke of the old friends who came to visit and to read to her and of the benefits of solitude, which enabled her to enjoy new insights into her life.

INSIGHT

Lucille hadn't expected this—that being here in the retirement home would bring sudden, uninvited benefits. She had been quite realistic in coming here and had told herself: "I'm quite blind; now I must go some place safe, where I'll be taken care of." She had stood one day in her garden, so lush that nearly every day of the year she could take a vase of fresh flowers to her office, and told herself she had to stop tripping on the steps and stumbling around in the dark, must give the house up, in fact. She knew others who had been happy here in Piedmont Gardens, so she signed herself in one day. She had imagined a slow, downward spiral, ever darkening in the descent.

Instead, her dream life had suddenly come alive. Jane Wheelwright said it, "Nature wants us to be balanced." If she couldn't see an inch before her nose, there was still her mind to bring her images.

She saw her sister in so many of the dreams, her older sister, about whom she had had such conflict. Perhaps the conflict had been all in herself, though, of course, Maurine had been aware of it. She had always wanted to be like beautiful Maurine, their parents' firstborn and their darling—ever correct, always good Maurine. Phi Beta Kappa too. No one could equal her. Lucille had resented her attitude for years, her terribly *good* attitude.

Just before their mother died, she told Lucille what the doctor had said when Lucille was born, "This is the *one.*" She said that Maurine, standing nearby, had heard him. Yet Maurine was always the one who had made Lucille feel guilty for never living up to her standard of goodness.

Maurine had been dead for almost a decade now. She had come to live with Lucille during her final illness; yet the ancient bitterness had remained unresolved. There was always so much work to do. All of Lucille's life the drawers of her mind were filled, it seemed—during medical school, during her training, then with her patients and her own trainees, and, of course, with her lover. It was no secret, the affair, at least as the years went on, even though he was married. Once a young woman came to interview her, and she told her that if she really wanted to understand her, she must know she had had a lover for many years, that love was central to her life. Dead now too, he also filled a large drawer in her mind and heart.

Then there had been the care of Elizabeth after her stroke. She owed so much to Elizabeth, who had analyzed her and helped her to train with Jung. They were strong friends throughout her career—of course, she had wanted to look after her at the end. Thoughts of her own family were stored into a narrow little drawer she seldom opened. Yet she cared for them all, for Libby, her niece who came to visit here, and Libby's children. It wasn't that she didn't care. The mind just hadn't grappled with this ancient rivalry.

In the unconscious mind, work was always going on. It released its knowledge in its own code and in its own time and resisted human time and theory.

"Too much theory," she had joked once to her friend Ann Miller as they walked along the beach at Carmel during a conference. Ann had said, "You're such a good antidote to it all, Lucille." Ann, who came to visit her in the home regularly, had always enjoyed laughing with her and appreciated her resistance to those who wanted to enshrine Jung's theory as something apart from the evolution of the mind itself. Ann would see the humor in what was happening to her now; Ann would see the wisdom of the unconscious too, helping her see after she was stone-blind into that sibling stranglehold of childhood. No matter how much we know about ourselves, there is always another drawer to open. Didn't Oedipus blind himself with his mother's brooch even after knowledge had overtaken him?

In the hallway a woman sat in her wheelchair, speaking in a loud defiant voice, "No, I won't; no, I won't; no, I won't; no, I won't . . . " The words lost their meaning after a while. A nursing home could teach you the value of a mantra—to empty the mind of emotional attachment. People might accuse the nurses of lacking compassion, but they were skilled at not being infected by negative emotion. That "stuck" person in the hall—she kept chanting. Lucille was skilled at distancing herself; yet something happened to her suddenly.

Outside her window was a patio, she had been told, made of concrete, with potted plants, a swath of grass. Visible to her was only the light, a shimmering square. And there her sister's image as a young mother appeared. A dream that Maurine had told her when she was ill and staying with her enacted itself there in the patio. Maurine's infant child had just died, and her husband as well. Maurine stood to the right, and between her and her husband lay a green valley. Far to the left he was to join her but was somehow detained. In her grief Maurine could not cry. The valley gave way before her, and there in front of her lay an enormous hole of tremendous depth. She knew that if she cried she would fall into the hole. She turned toward Lucille and held out her hands in an appeal. That appeal was not part of the original dream, but Lucille saw it now and realized the appeal. Her sister had never, never cried. A good person didn't cry, shouldn't. And Maurine had to be absolutely good because she was not the *one*.

A sense of tenderness for her sister flooded her, and gratitude, as that square of light created a mandala for her. Relief, happiness, and, finally, laughter. "I feel very dumb that I didn't see this before," she said out loud.

Here she was, an old woman in a nursing home, only now fully understanding this. Still cashing in on her analysis, it felt like. Hadn't she always said to her patients that the process was ever ongoing?

Such a simple insight, of the sort she'd helped hundreds of people to make. She herself had to go blind before she could see. She had always known that every darkness was the other side of a certain light, that the nether world existed to complement the whole. One door closes and another opens.

Lidia Puente Fielschmidt

Born February 8, 1907

Although Lidia Fielschmidt was a teacher for many years, she says she learned some of her best lessons late in life. She was born in San Salvador and was in school, as she puts it, from the age of five until thirty-seven, when she immigrated to the United States. She earned her teaching degree at seventeen, taught school in Sonsonate, and was the principal of a private girls' school for some years.

Almost immediately after she immigrated, her courtship with Joseph Fielschmidt began, although they did not speak one another's language. They were married in 1945 and have one child, a son, who is a chemist with Standard Oil. Many of Lidia's friends are former pupils from El Salvador who come to visit her, as do her sisters.

She was fifty-eight when she passed a Civil Service exam and went to work at the post office in San Francisco. There those late-life lessons began, an education in certain realities of American culture. But Lidia was still a teacher too.

LISTENING

Istood against the wall because all the seats in the hall were taken. A woman next to me, her white face riddled with anxiety, said, "Thank God you're here. Let's keep our backs to the wall." Suddenly I realized what the woman meant—the two of us were the only white people in a room of nearly one hundred applicants for the Civil Service exam. She meant, thank God there's another white person here. "If this is what it's like," she said, "I don't think I want a job at the post office." What the woman didn't realize was that I was Hispanic, from El Salvador.

The door burst open; desk seats were brought for the standees, and soon the examination was under way.

I hadn't realized my back was to the wall; but that was how I had felt in deciding to take the exam, driven to the wall by my own worries, which certainly had nothing to do with fear of other races but rather with demons in my mind. For some time my son had had a medical problem the doctors were unable to diagnose.

"You have to stop worrying," a friend had told me. "He will be well in good time." But somehow, because he was my only child, I felt possessed by guilt, as if his sickness were my fault. I hadn't worked since I married, but I was willing to try anything. When I saw the announcement about the exam, I decided to try.

It had been more than twenty years since I had worked, not since I was married, but I had no trouble with the test. After all, I'd been a teacher all those years in Sonsonate. A private school, a private life I had led. Married to my protective Joe, who only reluctantly agreed to let me work now.

Sheltered, that was how I felt, learning my new job there among all those streetwise black people. There had been no blacks in Sonsonate, only Indians. My family was middle-class. My father ran a pharmacy, but we were not wealthy. My mother ironed the clothes my three sisters and I wore. She loved ironing, she said, always had those crisp white dresses for us, had starched and ironed the white cotton sheets. The family never wanted for anything.

In the post office I learned what real want was, and understood for the first time the country I had adopted. El Salvador came into a deeper understanding for me too—my beautiful country with its violent nature and somber people, people who are so much more fatalistic than this good-humored black race.

My partner was Kay, at the rear dispatch. I myself worked the front register window. "She's so regal, like a queen," Joe said when Kay came for lunch one day. She was tall and elegant, towering over me. Kay told me she once had an inferiority complex and used to be quick to catch any slight against her race. Now she knew nobody was going to make her life better but herself, never mind which race she was.

I began to learn the stories of the others as they talked on the job. Like that white job applicant, they saw me as being like themselves. I have olive skin, and my hair, already gray, had a crimp in it.

Josepha, a stout girl at the next window, made a comment one day about a rather surly white customer, "White folks don't have troubles."

I said, "You're joking." I had begun to appreciate the humor of my co-workers, who talked freely in my presence about whatever was on their minds.

There was plenty on their minds, and not much of it a joke. I knew how to listen.

That had always been my strength as a teacher and a friend, hearing others. Even nowadays, children run up to my bench in the park and start telling me stories.

What I heard in the post office took my mind off my own troubles as nothing had before. Here were problems such as I had never imagined. Denise was from Louisiana, a woman of fifty with eight children, one a nightclub singer, one an artist in Paris, another in the hospital with polio since he was six, one who had run away, and, worst of all, one who was a murderer. "How do you handle all that?" I asked her. She answered, "As it comes, each day. I am proud of my daughter who sings, but that doesn't mean I am ashamed of my son who is in San Quentin. I go to see him. We talk. He is still my son." Then there was young Jana, not much more than twenty, who apparently was pregnant. She had three children and had been deserted by her husband. The baby on its way had been fathered by one of the mail carriers, married. And there was Maria, a very intelligent woman, determined to improve her life, whose children, twenty, twenty-two, and twenty-four, were unwilling either to go to school or to work. "I've had about all I can take," she said to me. And there was Clara, whose son, seventeen, had shot a police officer after an attempt he and some friends made at sticking up a bank in San Francisco.

These griefs unfolded over a period of some weeks, and I began to realize how sheltered my life had been. Why should I be privileged not to suffer? I realized, as my son got better, how wrapped up in my own troubles I had been. I grew to love the people I worked with.

Partly it was the laughter. The laugh no other people have. Somebody drops a packet of letters, spills them all over the floor, and there's a joke about it. Jana's child is born, and it isn't just a child—it's triplets. Now she has six children. Connie, the office organizer, creates a beautiful party for her, and Jana cracks jokes about what has happened to her—*six* fatherless children now. It was amazing, their spirit, I thought. I wished the woman who had been so apprehensive at the test could have gotten to know these intelligent, good-humored people.

Jana's story had a happy ending: the minister in her church fell in love with her, and their engagement was announced. Six children didn't frighten him.

One day Maria, who had the three thankless children, disappeared. She had been a model employee; it wasn't like her not to give notice. One of her children came looking for her on the job, saying she hadn't been home either. "She come back here, you tell her we need the rent." That seemed to be the end of Maria. Months passed, and there was no word. Then one day a postcard came to Kay, with no return address. Maria had a job on the East Coast as an executive secretary with a big increase in pay. "My kids don't know where I am," she added. "I'll check up on them in a couple of years to see if they ever got themselves together."

"Gut—sy," Josepha said. "Bet her boss be white though." Josepha herself had small children, said she wanted to tell them about Maria's example as an object lesson.

More than any of the others, Josepha continued to express a strong antagonism to white people. It was a routine with her. I wasn't sure how deep it went. Josepha could turn her round face from a smile to a scowl in less than a moment. Sometimes I heard an Amen echo Josepha's remarks.

I pondered it for some time. The people I worked with had helped me let go of my own worry. I felt released now in so many ways that I wondered if I could help

Josepha release her own obsession.

One day Josepha said, "I won't let my children play with whitey, that trash."

At that I decided to risk it. I asked, "Josepha, would you work with a white person?"

"Naw, not if I could help it."

"You get along all right with me, don't you?" It was true, the girl conceded. "But you're Hispanic."

I tried to explain to her that I was white where I came from. The members of my family were the equivalent of any of those white professionals Josepha was so scornful of. I said, "You are doing a disfavor to your child, passing on the inheritance of hate."

Josepha made a face at me and said nothing more. But that was the last time I heard her make a racial slur. Maybe she even stopped doing it at home.

I remained friends with these women long after I retired from my job. I had gone there thinking the work would distract me, but it had done much more. I had discovered a treasure of affection.

Virginia Walsh

Born December 29, 1907

Virginia Walsh watched the development of two generations of children under the treatment of the pediatrician Dr. Dorothy Orr, for whom she worked. Since her retirement, elders have benefited from her compassionate nature. Working through an organization called LITA (Love is The Answer), which operates in many cities of the Bay Area, pairing volunteer visitors with nursing-home residents, she has for many years paid visits to the confined.

Born in Denver, Virginia went to Rogers Hall School in Boston and Parsons Art School. She married a naval officer in 1931, and they lived in thirty-five different houses while raising their three daughters. Each of her daughters had a son, all of whom live near her. She lives alone in Marin County on a street that winds up to a view of the Bay. The view expands as you climb the stairs to her charming house. Although you may feel a little winded by the climb, the stairs present no difficulty to Virginia, thanks to her rigorous exercise program of yoga and aerobics, a class every day.

The story she told about one of the women she befriended through LITA is an especially chilling object lesson.

ENCOURAGEMENT

Virginia pulled into the nursing-home parking lot beside the ravine that sloped down to the Bay, thinking of the yoga precepts her teacher always mentioned: strength and flexibility. At seventy-six she was glad to be reminded that without those two assets you might wind up in a Golden Meadows Nursing Home, or some less friendly place. This was one of the most expensive in the county, a private institution that took no state-supported clients. Many of the rooms had a "bay view."

"I'd go batty visiting there," her friend in yoga class had said. "How can you stand it?" She told her about Laura, almost one hundred years old. "No one ever visits her," she said. "It's something I can do."

Laura hated Golden Meadows. She always asked Virginia to take her away. Virginia often found her in a different room. As other patients came and went, the management shifted Laura from room to room like an old chair. She had no possessions, only a picture of her husband.

Next week Laura would be one hundred years old. A one hundredth birthday shouldn't be simply passed over, Virginia thought; notice should be taken. She decided she would telephone Laura's family, speak with someone about her birthday. The nurse had told her the family was wealthy and that in the five years of Virginia's visits no family member had ever come to see her.

Today someone was there. A young girl with straight brown hair and wide uneasy eyes stood beside the wheelchair. "Our sorority is making visits," the girl explained. She had given Laura a gift, a teddy bear, which Laura hugged to her heart with emaciated hands, her thin face burrowing into the top of the bear's fuzz.

"What a wonderful idea to give her a bear," Virginia said. Laura rocked her toy. Suddenly she looked down the hallway and made a loud, plaintive cry. "Marianne, Joanna . . ."

"Her sisters' names," Virginia explained to the girl. "She probably wants them to look at her toy." The wail of her voice reverberated in the hall as if across a deep valley.

"They never come," Laura whined. Virginia had no idea if her sisters were even alive.

"We're here," Virginia said. "Your friends."

The girl looked frightened. She gripped her handbag so tightly her knuckles were white. That rise and fall in Laura's voice could strike terror if you weren't used to it. "I guess I'll go now you're here," said the girl, edging toward the door.

"I never thought of giving her a toy like that," Virginia said. "Come again. She needs all the company she can get."

"Good-bye," said the girl. Tears started in her big brown eyes. She glanced again at the bear, ducked her head, and fled.

Laura switched on the motor of her chair, which jerked away from Virginia. "Wait for me, Laura," Virginia followed her, amused as always at how fast she could make it go when she wanted to. Laura called back at her. "No, you're no good. You never take me home."

But in a few minutes they were sitting quietly in the sunroom. Laura reached out a hand for Virginia to hold; clutching her bear in the other hand, she rocked back and forth. "I'm going to escape from this jail," she said. "Swim to Alcatraz."

Virginia looked at her in astonishment. "Tell me about it." She knew that in her youth Laura had done just that, had been known as a long-distance swimmer. But Laura now lapsed into a long, disconnected ramble.

At the nurse's station Virginia dialed Laura's daughter. She had spoken with her once before, just to tell her she was making weekly visits. When the woman heard who it was, her voice tightened, as it had the other time. "Oh . . . yes." Not a question, but an imperative: Please be brief; I'm busy. Virginia thought the daughter must be about her own age. She told her what she had in mind: a little celebration at the nursing home, with perhaps some members of Laura's family? A notice in the paper then? After all, the family was well known in the area. And, also, Virginia went on, there was Laura's history, her famous swim to Alcatraz. "She spoke of it to me today." Virginia liked to imagine Laura in her twenties, mastering the frigid water in a voluminous wool bathing costume. A triumph worth mentioning when a person reaches one hundred.

"No, the family thinks that's inappropriate, given her condition. Thank you for calling. Good-bye."

Virginia hung up the silent instrument. Who knew, who could tell exactly what Laura's true condition was? Laura herself, the best witness, gave few clues, except for her frequently expressed desire to go home.

The nurse had a theory about the family. "I used to think that all of Laura's money had been eaten up by this place and that now they were having to dig into their own. But now I think it's worse. I think they've given it out that she's already dead. That way they don't have to admit they never come here."

Virginia shook her head. Perhaps it was too painful for the daughter to see her mother now. She knew how it would hurt her own daughters if she were in Laura's place. People did react differently to helplessness. Perhaps one reason she wanted Laura's birthday to be noticed was the beautiful party her own family had given her on her seventy-fifth birthday—her daughter's house was completely cleared of furniture, tables laid with pink cloths. Her sister even flew in from Denver. And little David gave a skit in which he played a sheik who whispered in her ear, "Come with me to the Casbah," mixing up movies he probably never saw, except in TV clips. They had put together a whole slide show of her from baby pictures through to that picnic last summer, in a takeoff on "This Is Your Life." She was loved—*that* was the answer to how she could bear to make her visits to Laura.

A few weeks after Laura's birthday, Virginia found her in the infirmary. She had finally tried to make her escape, the nurse told her. She had raced her chair through the automatic front doors and into the parking lot, where it skidded down the ravine. She might have fallen straight into the Bay except for the cyclone fencing.

Her forehead was bandaged where it had been cut in the fall, and she was very badly bruised.

"But why is she in that strange position?" Virginia asked, for Laura lay with her feet up in the air, although, with her eyes closed, she seemed to be asleep.

Laura's eyes snapped open. "I'm willing my body to science," she said quite lucidly. "They'll find it interesting. My legs will not unbend."

In the hallway Virginia asked the nurse what could be done about Laura's legs. Surely some physical therapy? The nurse compressed her lips. The family had stopped the physical therapy, said they had no medical-insurance coverage for it.

Virginia left to go to her yoga class, where again her friend commented on her visits to the nursing home. "You're too good," she said almost reproachfully.

They were just finishing Savasana, the corpse pose, lying outstretched in relaxation.

Lilias on TV liked to call it by a euphemism, the sponge, but its Sanskrit meaning was corpse pose. The yogis knew what they were doing: a practice for death, for surrender of one's life, could make it easier in the end.

Frances Mary Albrier

Born September 21, 1898

Frances Albrier was blessed with strong teachers from early childhood, first her half-Irish grandmother and her Black-foot Indian grandfather who raised her in Tuskegee, Alabama, then the great educators of Tuskegee: Booker T. Washington and George Washington Carver.

She received a bachelor's degree from Howard University in 1920 and moved to California. There she married an engineer, William Albert Jackson, who died in 1930. While raising their three children, she worked as a practical nurse and a housemaid. As a maid for the Pullman Company, she supported the creation of the Brotherhood of Sleeping Car Porters. She married Willie Albrier, a Pullman bartender, in 1934.

During the thirties and forties she became active politically, was the first woman elected to her county and state Democratic central committee. She was the first black person hired by Kaiser Shipyards during World War II. She agitated successfully for the hiring of the first black teachers in California.

In her later years she has dedicated herself to problems of the elderly. She attended the White House Conference on Aging in 1971, and her vision made the three model senior centers in Berkeley a realization. What she told us about her grandmother demonstrates how moral strength is passed from one generation to the next.

BREAKING GROUND

Someone handed Frances a little shovel, trimmed in Christmas red and green. She was supposed to turn the first shovelful of earth for the new senior centers. Despite a threatening December sky, they would have three ground-breaking ceremonies that afternoon—if need be, up to their ankles in mud.

Suddenly an image of her grandmother, spading in her garden, appeared before her. There in Tuskegee, Grandma always made two rows: one for her family and one for anybody. Because she knew people would come and take things out of the garden, she always provided for them. Frances had come a long way since her Tuskegee childhood, but it was never very far from her mind.

She was older now than her grandmother had lived to be, and as she stood in Berkeley, with all the city officials and the people who had worked with her on the centers, it was as if her grandmother were with her again. She looked around at the elders who wore little yellow buttons saying, "Count us in"—Asians, blacks, Hispanics, whites. As a model city for integration, Berkeley played the old "steps" game, and the giant steps weren't always forward.

A reporter from the *Gazette* approached her. How had she gotten the centers started?

Maybe she had begun thinking about it a long time ago. There wasn't any concern about the aged in her grandmother's day. She told the reporter she had worked in hospitals and had seen elders mistreated and misunderstood. She had worked on the community board that discovered that many people were undernourished because they lived alone and never got out, so she got busy doing something about it.

"Was this easier than some of your other battles, Mrs. Albrier?" To tell the truth, it was a whole lot easier.

There wasn't any counting-us-in going on when she first came to town. Her life here had been a series of confrontations.

Grandma had taught her how to confront any situation and how to understand it. When Frances was twelve, Grandma decided to send her to Europe with a wealthy white woman, Lelia Schwartz, whom she had reared at the end of the Civil War and who needed a maid she could trust. "She'll take care of you," Grandma insisted, "and will give you an education abroad." Six feet tall, Grandma was hard to resist, and reluctantly Frances agreed to go.

In the Louvre in Paris, Mrs. Schwartz tipped the attendant, saying, "This is my girl; you show her everything." He did. In England Mrs. Schwartz's butler took her through all the old castles, and they listened to all of that horrible history. And one day the butler took her to factories where they made cloth. There she saw hundreds of poor children, some of them in rags or G-strings, weaving the cloth along with the grown people. She and the butler saw how the people lived in darkness: dark rooms, dark streets. And when she got home, her grandmother met the confusion created in the child's mind.

"I saw people working in one part of the city, and in the other part were Mrs. Schwartz and her friends, all refined and polished; and you want me to be like them. Mrs. Schwartz has a $10,000 necklace and thought nothing of throwing it down, didn't take care of it. But the poor people—they were nice and kind and grateful if I gave them money. If I was God, I wouldn't have that. I'd take some of the money away from these rich people and give it to those people slaving in the factories. There must not be no God," she declared.

Grandma hated to see Frances turn against God and become vindictive toward white people. She said, "I should have prepared you for what you would see in traveling: the poor people, the struggling people. It isn't God's doing; it's people misusing what God put on earth. You have to realize that these things exist and that you can help change them. Instead of challenging God, you have to find ways to challenge people. You can help them to change."

That understanding was the power behind Frances in everything she had done. Grandma's philosophy backed her up at Kaiser Shipyards in World War II. She had gone to welding school for the sixty hours of training required by Kaiser, then took sixty more. She had to be better than others who were hunting jobs because she was a black woman. Finally her instructor sent her to Kaiser. She passed the welding test easily, so she went to join the union.

She stood in line, but when her turn came, the man at the window said they couldn't accept a black woman into the union. Four servicemen were standing in the hall, two white and two black. They started yelling, "Is this the democracy we're being drafted to fight for? The first thing we should do is tear up this hall." She thanked them, but said to hold on; she was going to talk to the chairman of Kaiser Shipyards.

Frances gave the chairman's receptionist a lecture. She said that if there was discrimination at the shipyard, she was there to ask them to change it. She was there to respond to a call from the government to help build Victory Ships. She spoke with calm and reason. Her grandmother would have liked it. The chairman of the company came out and listened to her too, then sent her over to the director of the union, who saw that she got the first card ever issued to a black woman. It was a start, but it wasn't enough. They let her in to shut her up; she was the first and only black person for a time. Later they let in a few black men. There was a lot more work to do.

There at the ground-breaking ceremony a splatter of rain touched her shoulder. Why had this project been so easy? It was true, the seniors had met for some time in an inadequate space, but once she heard that matching funds were available and spoke to Judge Ramsey, he helped her find the funds. The money for the centers had come forth as if through some stroke of magic. Three-and-a-half million dollars. No conflict, no struggle. It wasn't at all characteristic; it broke the pattern of her life.

They would dedicate the land, and soon the modern buildings would house all the activity she had worked for: hot lunches in pleasant dining rooms, useful classes, legal and health services. She would be there as community liaison, making sure people knew they didn't have to sit home all day and eat alone; they could get out and find friends.

She bent down, dug the little shovel into the dirt, and tossed the first spadeful of rain-softened earth. *Two rows, one for anybody.*

The whole crowd joined her in a cheer. It was true—no real conflict over creating these buildings. People could see themselves in another person's situation now so much better than when she was small. There was no more child labor in England. The centers stood for an idea whose time had come. People were beginning to understand that if they lived, they, too, would be old someday.

Josephine Enizan Araldo

Born January 31, 1897

From her grandmother in Brittany, Josephine Enizan developed a love of the table, a passion for garden freshness in cuisine, and a sense of surprise. Grandmère used to mix cherries with string beans, kumquat with chard, turnips with figs. From the age of seven until she was twenty, she worked in her grandmother's garden and helped in the kitchen. They were "land rich," and Josephine remembers that their bathroom was the river, where she and her seven sisters and brothers took their baths.

She went to Paris to work for the Louis Loucheur family, who paid her tuition to the Cordon Bleu. Every morning before school she went to mass, then attended classes all day; and every evening she prepared meals for the Loucheur family. When she wasn't busy, she says, she would go with the master chef Henri-Paul Pellaprat to his country house to help him with dinner parties. She received her diploma in 1923, and Pellaprat gave her a toque blanche, crowning her chef.

The following year the Mortimer Fleishhacker family invited Josephine to become their chef in San Francisco. Since then she has worked for many prominent families in San Francisco, as well as for celebrated visitors such as Lily Pons, who always arranged far in advance of the opera season for Josephine to cook for her.

In 1925 she met Charles Araldo, a vaudeville accordionist. Josephine proposed to him, and they were married at Notre Dame des Victoires by a priest who for years afterward enjoyed the reward of the frequent meals that Josephine prepared for him and others in his order. When she began to teach cooking, Charles helped by preparing an herb garden and by playing the accordion after the dinners her students made and joyously consumed.

After Charles's death in 1983, Josephine went to live with their daughter, Jacqueline, and her four children. One of her many enthusiastic students, Mary Pitts, used to send copies of recipes from cooking class to another student, a "Josephine addict," who had moved away.

NOURISHMENT

Dear Donna,

Here are today's recipes. I stopped off and had them photocopied for you after class. We cooked today: Tourtière Poitevine (pork pie with chicken liver, pork, and onion), Courgettes à la Crème (zucchini), and Sabayon Froid. Josephine is happy to have me send these recipes to you.

She caught me with one of her sudden questions today...

Mary hadn't planned to get deeply into haute cuisine. She hadn't even wanted to go to Josephine's class when Donna had first suggested it. "We'll just take her Fundamentals course," Donna had insisted. Only ten classes, each one devoted to a different aspect of French cuisine: soup one week, salads the next, then eggs, then sauces and their derivatives. "Doesn't that sound useful?"

Mary had protested. She was kitchen-bound enough with her two children. This sounded like an even heavier commitment. Getting *out* of the kitchen was more what she had in mind, but finally she went along with Donna.

From the moment she and Donna entered Josephine's funky kitchen, they knew there wasn't anybody like her. They'd expected a more orderly immaculate kitchen, a *Sunset* magazine image with carefully arranged spice jars and gleaming copper pots. But, there, beside an ancient gas stove, stood tiny Josephine in her white apron, with her white chef's hat ballooning over her head. One of her eyes, Mary realized, was made of glass.

The shelves rising behind Josephine were jam-packed with household clutter she must have had for years—photos with curled corners sticking out at odd angles, balls of string, plastic bags, curious jars filled with things Mary didn't recognize at first. A diagram of a side of beef, labeled in French, hung from a wall; and framed slogans were propped up here and there, with one saying: "Don't let anything dampen your spirits." A board, carefully carved in calligraphy— "Sacramento, California"—was mystifying. They soon learned its significance, however.

The eight students crowded into a tiny breakfast nook, opposite the table where Josephine had laid out the food to be prepared. At such close quarters at least they wouldn't miss anything.

Her energy would have carried in the Masonic Temple. She was impassioned, fierce, humorous. She started off showing them how to make a fundamental pâte, briskly beating egg yolks and singing a ronde as she worked. It was what she always sang for beating eggs and sauces, she said, a song of her teacher at the Cordon Bleu, M. Pellaprat.

Et pendent ce temps là (And all the while)

Je tournais la manivelle (I was turning the crank)

Et monsieur jouait de la prunelle (He was making eyes at me)

Comme un gros pacha.   (Like a fat pasha.)

Nothing to do with sauces, after all, but just the right rhythm for beating. After she rolled out the dough for the pâte, she checked her oven. "I always put in the oven a brick," she said. "It keeps steady the temperature."

A young man moved to help clean up the breadboard, but she stopped him. Students did not help in Josephine's kitchen. Besides, you did not throw anything away.

These flour crumbs you must save—so. And down from the shelf came one of those mysterious jars, into which she scraped the flour shreds. For thickening gravy, she explained. "It has already the butter in it." The jars, Mary realized, were filled with cake crumbs, bread crumbs, apple skins. Frugality was essential to Josephine's cuisine.

"Sacramento, California!" she cried out suddenly. "Where is that gigolo? He was to bring fruit for us to have with this." She pointed to her sign "Sacramento, California." She had adopted this geographical euphemism years ago to substitute for "sacrebleu," when one of her employers objected to her swearing. The "gigolo" was her beloved husband, Charles, who appeared on cue with a basket of fruit.

She fired this at me out of the blue, "Marie, what are the five aromatic herbs? Name them for us." She held her thumb in the air to count them off. Of course, I had to stammer around. Then her mock exasperation. You can feel such affection in Josephine at the same time she's letting you know how utterly important food, nourishment, is.

I wasn't the only one to get one of her impromptu quizzes—she fired at another returning student, "How much al–chol in the sauce? Exactement!" He was ready, though; he remembered Josephine's dictum: Enough that you can taste. Why put it in if you cannot taste!

They shared the food afterward, and Charles played the accordion for them. Josephine's dishes were always wonderful to eat, of course, but it was more than that. Josephine's kitchen had had an enhancing effect on Mary's life, for there she had learned more than cooking. She had learned the building blocks of a cuisine that had helped her bring ease into the rituals of food and eating, so that the occasions that bring people together, from breakfast to banquet, had become more joyful.

There was something about Josephine—an impish feeling that no bind was so strong that you couldn't, with a little wit, get out of it, set things right. Among the many stories she told about her former teachers and employers was the one about her first disaster. For a fancy party she had planned Riz à l'Impératrice for dessert, a tall Bavarian cream mold decorated with glacéed fruits to resemble a stained-glass window. When she unmolded the dish, it sank and looked like a pancake. But Josephine, remembering the motto she learned from M. Pellaprat—never let anything dampen your spirits—scooped the cream into glasses and decorated it with the fruits. She christened it Royal Flop.

Humor and optimism blended together with a spirit of cooperation. One day in class Mary noticed that Josephine's glass eye was not centered properly in its socket. A little later Josephine caught sight of herself in a mirror and turned to the class. "How come nobody tells me my eye is looking into space? You have to tell me—I don't want to be crooked."

She told us a little about her trip this summer in France, traveling on a Eurail Pass with a backpack (at eighty) to visit some out-of-the-way chefs. She told one of them he was paying too much for broccoli. She showed me the notebooks of what she'd learned on this trip as well as those she'd written other summers. They're piled floor to ceiling in a back room.

It wasn't just a positive attitude in the kitchen but in the whole of life. Even when she was in pain, as she had been much of last year, she said such things as, "I am good at standing pain; I am good at standing everything."

Donna, I wish you could be with us. Imagine, two years I've been in her advanced classes and she still hasn't repeated a menu! I'll send the recipes to you with my notes, but I have my doubts whether the dishes will really taste the same without the inspiration of Josephine herself.

    Love,

    Mary

Mary Frances Kennedy Fisher

Born July 3, 1908

When a venerated writer reaches a great age, she should be free, among other things, to choose where she wishes to live. For M.F.K. Fisher it is in the Valley of the Moon in Sonoma County, a peaceful geography easily accessible to her family and friends, in a house designed especially for her needs. She tells how this came about for her, and of her life in that house, in her essay "Nowhere but Here" in the collection As They Were.

In fact, she is best described in her own writing, which for five decades has attracted an ever-increasing readership, because of the unique personal quality of her work. Whether she is writing of her childhood, in Among Friends, *a loving memoir of her life in the Quaker community of Whittier, California, where her father, a non-Quaker, was the newspaper editor, or of her life abroad, as in* The Gastronomical Me, *which in a series of essays gives us glimpses of her first marriage, to Alfred Fisher, then a professor at the University of Dijon, France, and of their divorce and her subsequent remarriage and tragic widowhood, or whether she is writing about food—the preparation, serving, and enjoyment of it—or of her feelings about aging, in* Sister Age, *the reader savors her presence like that of a humorous, brilliant, and courageous friend who never tells us more than we want to know. If her work is about "the good life," there is also an ideal of goodness that informs it, as well as a wealth of learning and experience that always touches the spirit. When asked why she writes about food and hunger, the subject of so many of her essays that first appeared in the* New Yorker, *she said, "There is a communion of more than our bodies when bread is broken and wine is drunk."*

Recently the West Coast publishing house, North Point Press, known for its distinguished list, reissued two of her books long out of print: A Cordiall Water *and her only novel,* Not Now, but Now; *and so all seventeen of her books are now available.*

In 1964 three civil rights workers, James Schwerner, Michael Chayney, and Andrew Goodman, disappeared in Mississippi and were later found murdered. At that time M.F.K. Fisher happened to be teaching at a private school for blacks near Jackson, having volunteered for a year and a half. In her midfifties then, she had been divorced from her third husband, the book editor Donald Friede; and their two daughters, Kennedy and Anna, were then on their own. She was the youngest volunteer the school had ever had. She herself has not written of this episode in her life, but here is the story she told about it.

BIRDS OF PASSAGE

Lor some months Mary Frances was the only white volunteer at the school. When she arrived, the school director and founder, Dr. J., said that the other white women who taught as volunteers would flock down from the north later like migrant birds.

Helicopters were swarming about the property, and at either end of the campus lookout towers were manned with armed black guards. Dr. C., a white woman who ran the school's office and was the director's assistant, ignored her question about them, showed her instead the schedule of high school classes she would teach—from six in the morning until nine-thirty at night. Attendance at daily chapel and Sunday morning services in the assembly were also expected. Dr. C., who knew of her reputation as a writer, appeared to view her with suspicion, as if she might want to write something about their school for the northern bias.

When she got to her room, a young black student, Beatrice, brought sheets. She told Mary Frances she was getting her junior college degree in "laundry." This was a work school—all the students, from kindergartners through junior college students, earned their way. Beatrice must know everything going on if, after mornings at the mangle, she delivered sheets all over the school, but she couldn't explain the helicopters still swarming like giant swamp mosquitoes.

Her students, she soon realized, had the habit of averting their eyes from any white person's. In the dining hall, a long walk, half a mile from her room, the black teachers were noncommittal about the helicopters. A striking old woman, lean and hawklike, with blue black skin, sat apart; she wore starchy white. "Dr. Nell," someone said, "the school nurse. She treats with yarbs." There must have been Indian in her, Choctaw maybe. An herbal witch doctor. The woman's gaze roved the room, watchful, assessing. Mary Frances felt overcome with shyness.

The food was unbelievably bad: pone, white beans, and creamed corn, nothing green. No wonder the teachers were nearly all overweight. In the kitchen she could see a five-gallon can of corn, newly opened. She tasted everything—only the corn was palatable, with a little salt.

Why had she come here? After seeing her father through the final days of his illness, she had put his newspaper to bed for the last time. The house on the old ranch where she grew up, in ruins, had been bulldozed and the property given to the city of Whittier according to Father's will. For the first time in many years she was free, if homeless. She had always heard of this school in Mississippi. Mother used to send their castoff clothing here, anything that was still good. She knew the school depended on its volunteers. With her life so changed now, she wanted to put her own work aside for a time and do something entirely different.

It was only later in the teacher's room, where she overheard two old men, that she understood the helicopters. The men, masters in the boys' dormitories, failed to notice her reading in a corner. State officials were dragging the nearby swamps, looking for three missing white civil rights workers who had come down from New York to register voters. They had found one body—a black youth whose family hadn't seen him since Christmas. The guards, she realized, would be watching for rednecks on a rampage against the school. The men exchanged murmurs. "His mama claimed him. He was all cut up. The sheriff ask her why she don't put in a report before." The scene presented

itself in her mind: a black woman gazing at her mutilated son who would never have been sought, never found, except for this search for white strangers.

She flung herself into learning how to teach, which she had never done before. The texts were out-of-date castoffs from white schools. But among them she found a gem of an old anthology of American literature from Cotton Mather's time up to about 1910. With that she started to work on her students' language.

They spoke three languages as far as she could tell: their private family language, their school language, and the language they thought whites wanted them to speak. She couldn't understand the private language at all, imagined she wasn't meant to. To strengthen their "school" language, she gave them James Baldwin's *The Fire Next Time*, with its "Burn, baby, burn" message; she told them Black Is Beautiful. That brought objections from Dr. C. in the office: this was not a radical school, could not afford to be thought so by the white community. But the director, Dr. J., gave her permission to start a school newspaper. That would give her students a chance to write their personal language, knowing it would be published and read by all the school.

The hardest work was to get the students to laugh. Whenever she was the least humorous, their minds seemed to be asleep in clover fields. Slowly she learned the rules. No laughing in front of a white person. No showing any feelings anytime. She learned also that the school had a spy system: word of anything out of line found its way back to the front office, and swift punishment ensued. Laughter *with* a white teacher was far out of line.

She didn't think of herself as white—pink maybe, with the humid air flushing her sensitive skin. Her students were every color, from white to violet black. The blackest was B., a sixteen-year-old African from Lambaréné in Gabon, sent to the school on a scholarship by the American Legion. As the only person in the school who knew French, Mary Frances helped him in his own language until his skimpy English improved. Disdainful of his "racially corrupted" classmates, he made few friends, despite considerable charm and cleverness. He had an uncanny way of using a pencil, could draw airplanes practically to scale merely from having seen them fly overhead. He had a terrifying ambition: to learn enough English to join the U.S. Air Force and be trained as a pilot, then to return to his own country to become its dictator. The school assigned him to the garbage detail—punishment for naughtiness.

One day, from her classroom window, she glimpsed B. at his appointed task. An old mule was hitched to the garbage cart, which was set on high, colorfully painted wheels. He stood in the cart as if it were a chariot, flourishing a whip over the head of the apathetic mule. The energy of his solitary fantasy made Mary Frances burst out laughing. "Well, *look* at him," she insisted to her class. "He's so jaunty!" He flourished his whip again, and the mule, startled out of its lethargy, took him and the cart racing away. The laughter bubbled up, low and satisfying.

Within a few weeks the swamp had yielded the bodies of five black men. Each time the families of the murdered men came to claim them. A pall fell over the school as the search for the missing white civil rights workers went on.

A few more white volunteers arrived, all of them old women in their eighties. In the dining hall over a bowl of creamed corn, all that Mary Frances could eat of the fare, she got to know them. One was planning to organize the library for the junior college students; she had raised five children in a sod hut in the plains after being deserted by her husband. Now she had glaucoma but was returning for her second year at the school. Another was the kindergarten teacher, inarticulate with adults but fluent in kid talk, crippled by arthritis. And there was Ethel, whose diet kept her out of the dining hall; she cooked on a wood stove in her room, for her diabetes. None of them was well; yet they came here year after year, brave, dedicated, old women. A Scottish woman arrived, Dr. McG.— one of those small, compact, powerful women, also in her eighties, head of a community hospital in upstate New York; she wanted to learn of health conditions in the south.

Dr. McG. won the confidence of the old yarb woman. Partly because of Dr. Nell's remoteness from other whites, it was a pleasure to Mary Frances to see the two of them together, the tall black woman and the small Scottish woman, warm and interested in everything. Dr. McG., respectful of the yarb woman, taught only hygiene and child care. Never offering prescriptions, she preferred to learn what she could of Dr. Nell's violent teas, her swamp medicine and midwifery.

The students had printed the first issue of the newspaper and delivered it to the director, who, walking with Mary Frances between classes, congratulated her on improvement in the students' writing. They could begin to sell the paper the next day.

In the school store, which was always scantily stocked, Mary Frances bought Kraft caramels and ice cream. At first she had a quarter of a pint of ice cream a day, but because she was eating only creamed corn at mealtimes, she began to want more. In another life, people who read books thought of her as an artist for what she wrote about nourishment, what it means to the spirit and the conduct of life for a dish to be thoughtfully prepared, presented, and shared. Partaking of culinary delight—that was her metaphor. What would her readers think if they knew that nowadays visions of ice cream in cardboard containers rose before her and that she feasted voluptuously upon it alone in her room at night?

At the school office a shock awaited her. The white assistant, Dr. C., and her helpers had censored the paper. She stared at their handiwork, stunned. Each of the newspapers lay in lacy shreds. This was impossible for her to take in at first. She had grown up in a newspaper household; censorship was unthinkable. She stared at Dr. C., incredulous. "We took out a few things that tended to put the school in a bad light," Dr. C. told her.

Mary Frances left the office with the mutilated newspapers. In her classroom she and the horrified students examined them together. One boy's story about the first football game he had ever attended was demolished. He had written, "I was so scared my palms were white." Dr. C. had cut "my palms were white." He wrote of his homesickness: "I wish I could be at home and not in school." That, too, had been cut, along with any other phrase that suggested feeling. His signature was intact, and the cuts made him look ridiculous. The censorship made a mockery of all the students who had worked so hard on the paper.

She apologized to them. "I'm so sorry. I think we shouldn't put it on sale."

They agreed and fell silent. They could see how shaken she was by what the woman had done. One of the older boys said, "We're used to this, but you're not."

Appeals began from the students to help them escape. Because of the spy system, she had never been able to schedule private conferences with them, but now they sought her out furtively. Beatrice, the "laundry" major, asked for help in her plan to go to California. A young man who expected to get married after he got his degree told her he would kill himself if he had to stay in Mississippi. Could she help him move away?

She herself began to dream of flight. She longed to go to Jackson, to get on a plane. She would fly first class, she thought, and be served something like a cold, stuffed quail. She would drink champagne, forget this nightmare.

The next evening she left her creamed corn uneaten in the dining room. It was a sweltering night, and she felt she couldn't drag herself to her eight-thirty class. She would just go into the school store and buy ice cream, she thought, then leave the next day, fly away.

On the way back from the dining room, she overtook the old kindergarten teacher, hobbling with her arthritic hip. She said, "You don't have to walk with me; I'm pretty slow." Mary Frances asked if she was in pain.

She shook her head. "If you keep busy, you don't notice your aches and pains so much."

Mary Frances said nothing, except to herself, "You spoiled brat."

In class she read to her students, an essay by John Audubon from that ancient anthology, about a nighttime slaughter by frontier farmers of thousands of passenger pigeons, a bird now extinct, at their roosting place during a migration. "Their foes anxiously prepared to receive them. Some persons were ready with iron pots containing sulphur, others with torches of pine knots; many had poles and guns." Audubon wrote of the sound made by the immense flocks of birds, a sound heard for three miles around, like a hard gale at sea passing through the rigging of a vessel, so loud the gunfire could not be heard as the birds were felled, and of how the next day the farmers gathered as many birds as their families could eat in a season, then set loose hundreds of hogs to gorge on the pigeons still lying dead in the forest, and of the sunrise flight of the birds able to escape the massacre, flying on an altered course, passing toward extinction. When she finished and looked up, the students sat in a hush. Some had tears in their eyes for the vanished birds.

In her room she ate a pint of ice cream. Night sounds of crickets and frogs rose from the swamp. Moths flung their bodies at the light of her window; mosquitoes buzzed at the screen. She knew her sugary diet of creamed corn and ice cream was wrecking her teeth. One had already gone. "If you cannot swallow," she would write years later, "you are afraid of your enemy."

On Sunday she followed a flurry of large, black women in satin dresses and plumes into the assembly hall for chapel—where else could they wear their finery? The old yarb woman was there in her white silk dress. Mary Frances sat behind the row of white volunteers, whose gray hair was contained in silvery nets, like halos. Hymns moved the torpid air. The voices, both shrill and mellow, a vibrant mixture, sang of the crossing of rivers, of promised lands.

Stirred by the sorrowful songs, she sat alone after everyone else had filed out. When she stood up, someone grasped her arm. It was the old yarb woman. An alarm shot through her. She began to tremble. The yarb woman *never* touched a white person. Now she reached her bony hand up and took Mary Frances by the chin, gazing at her closely. At last she spoke. "You're good," she said. "You're good." And then she turned and went about her business.

Martha St. John

Born January 15, 1918

Once all of the San Francisco Bay Area, from San Jose north through the Carquinez Strait, was Indian territory, where American Indians fished the fresh water of the Bay in clear air, and, although they lived simply in small groups, they were united in a shared knowledge of the spirit. Today there are more than 56,000 Indians in that same geographical area who have left the poverty of reservations for uncertain economic prospects in the cities. A network of spiritual support still exists, and at its center is Martha St. John, whose life is dedicated to the preservation of the spirit of American Indian people.

Martha goes wherever she is called. Throughout that same ancient territory, she travels wherever there is a need for medicine, whether for body or spirit. When the Native American torchrunners were on their way to Los Angeles to salute the Olympic Games, Martha drove three hundred miles with special food she knew would give them energy and cooked it for them. Since she was widowed in her early sixties, she has become an elder, in the true sense of the word, to all her people. Hundreds of children call her Grandmother.

She was born a Sioux on the Sisseton Reservation on the northeast tip of South Dakota, where she married in 1930. It was some thirty years later that she and her husband left the reservation; she has come into this life of serving the urban tribes in her later years. She has eleven daughters—six of her own, five adopted—and four sons, two of whom are adopted.

Besides her work as medicine woman, she has taught other Americans as well. Starting in 1973, she worked as an instructional assistant in a parent-participant preschool program designed for American Indian children. Initially federally funded, the school became a children's center when funds were reduced, and Martha still does volunteer work there. She has taught the Sioux language to linguists at the University of

California at Berkeley and gives special lectures in the Native American Studies program on that campus. She is a frequent consultant at DQU, the accredited American Indian junior college near Davis, California, whose initials stand for the names of Iroquois and Aztec gods, signifying a union of tribal spirit.

We visited her at a sundance on the DQU campus, which is a former U.S. Army training ground in the middle of a barren field south of Sacramento. The dance took place in an arena encircled by a shaded arbor covered with woven willow branches. Thirty men were dancing, and eight women. The men, many of them youths in their teens and early twenties, were bare to the waist and deeply sunburned. They wore international colors representing the races: a red breechcloth appliquéd with yellow, black, and white. Over their dresses the women had tied colored shawls fringed with white. The men held reed whistles between their teeth, which they blew in rhythm to drums played at the side of the arena. In the center of the dancing arena stood the only tall tree on the entire campus, a high cottonwood festooned with bands of the international colors.

During the four days of their salute to the sun, the dancers remained in the arena apart from all others, retiring only for resting periods in a section of the shady arbor roped off for them, or to sleep at night in the tepees reserved for them. They also withdrew to sweat baths, inside canvas-covered huts.

Martha was very occupied, for she was cooking much of the food for the gathering of approximately two hundred people, and she was also called upon to take part in a ceremony of the dance. She moved with ease from kitchen work to conversation with us, to the dancing arena, and back to the kitchen again, frequently pausing to talk to people who stopped her momentarily for a word of advice.

HEALING

This dance is for all people of the earth, to heal them. It is a sacrifice.

Now it is a multinational dance. That is the meaning of the colors. The young boys pledge to live clean lives in the Indian way. This dance brings them back into the tribal life. They serve others between the dances: cleaning, serving food.

The cottonwood tree was cut down and brought here. It is planted in a hole dug deep enough to keep it straight. And beneath it is food for the great-grandparents, and medicine for their spirits as well.

One of the chief dancers signals me at the end of each dance to pass the pipe from their arena out to the musicians. They can pass the pipe to thank those who play for them, but throughout the four days they cannot step out of the circle marked off by red stakes. They call me and three others to pass the pipe for them. We four represent the four corners of the earth.

The song says:

I want to live with my great-grandfather;

But he is no longer alive.

Have pity on me.

When the men fan one of the dancers with the eagle feathers, that is to give the dancer power, to heal him.

The dance is a cleansing. You have to endure suffering to help others overcome it.

My husband was the one who had the healing power. I carry on the spirit that he gave to me. I had his medicine pipe, but a woman took it from me, saying a woman had no right to use it. It doesn't matter. I send the medicine through a reed to the person who is sick, blowing it onto the person's body, where the sickness is, and the healing takes place. I work on the center of the head much of the time because that is where a lot of the sickness comes from.

If old people are lonely and say everyone has left them and no one comes to see them, I say let them go. You do not have to have other people. You have the earth, the sun, the sky, the grass. You have yourself, and you can heal your mind by talking to the earth. Watch the grass, and you will learn how it grows from the earth and will be in touch again with the spirit that guides us.

We had a call to go once to San Jose, to a man with a bad cancer of the throat. He had been to a white doctor who told him he had to have an operation. He was losing his voice, becoming hoarser and hoarser. We gave him the medicine. That time I placed my reed on his throat and sucked through the reed. Suck more and suck harder, my husband said. He prayed all the time. Next day the man said, "I was very sick last night. I vomited all night long, and much blood and pus came up." Sure enough, when my husband looked into his throat, the cancer was not there. We told him to wait a while and he would be completely healed. The next week he had an appointment with the doctor, who said, "I know a cancer when I see one, and I know you had it. What has happened?" "Well," the man told him, "you know, there are Indians here, old people, who know old medicine. I won't tell you who they are, but they came and they helped me." Then the doctor said, "Well, there is still a small cancer here on the other side of your throat. We'll make an appointment to remove that." So the man came back to us, and we told him to wait another week. "You'll see, the medicine is still working. You won't have that small cancer either by next week." And so the doctor was surprised again.

We also went to heal a man of a bad heart. When I gave him the medicine, he was startled at first and knocked the pipe from my hand, but the medicine fell upon his body, so we knew that it would work, even if it had missed his heart. And he is well today.

I am not teaching this medicine. Someone may have a dream or a vision. Then she will come to me, will know. Then I can teach. We have visions all the time; they come to you and go so quickly that you lose them. You need to pay attention to such moments.

I have a problem with my sight, split vision. I know the herb that can heal that condition and where it is, but I have not yet gotten word that I may use it for myself. The spirit comes to me in dreams to direct my own healing. And so I must wait.

In the MacArthur Shopping Center my husband and I saw a wounded blackbird. He said, "Martha, pick him up, he is sick." I touched his head, checked his wing, his feet, and held him up in my hand and showed him the way. He flew off. Nothing was wrong with him.

My husband did not heal himself. He died of cancer. He was ready to die. I asked him, "Why are you ready to die when so many people need you?" He spoke of the young people who were smoking pot, of the people who were drinking, of the confusion created by living in the cities, of how so many young people no longer care about their heritage. He remembered the man running a store on a corner in our neighborhood. "For twenty years we traded there and didn't know he was half-Indian," my husband said. "He didn't care to tell us his true identity, didn't care to claim it." My husband felt things would get worse for the Indians, and he was ready to go. He was discouraged. He said he would leave it to me to carry on for him, to heal wherever I could.

The state did not give us this campus. We occupied it. They had to cede it to us finally under the treaty that says we may take back land once ours that has been abandoned. We had to work hard to have it accredited, and still they are trying to take it away.

I tell my students that the cultures have a common worth and are merging. They must learn all they can of the non-Indian culture so as to understand it, know how other people live and what they want, for knowledge is their only protection. I tell them to learn all they can of their own culture, to hang onto it and never forget. If they take on the burden of learning so much more than the non-Indians, then even in this merging they cannot become extinct.

The dancers go into the sweat baths, and there a woman asks, "How many stones?" She will chant as she pours water over the stones. Perhaps you want five or ten, or sometimes even thirty—the more stones, the hotter it is. I go into the baths too. They are suffering—I will suffer too. The sunburn will peel off and give them new skin, purified. The dancers are ready for us to pass the pipe again. The song says:

My grandfather is no longer alive;
That is why I am sad.
Bless me.

Margaret Calder Hayes

Born February 1, 1896

Peggy Calder was born in Paris in an artist's studio. Her father was the second of the Alexander Calders she wrote about in her perceptive family memoir, **The Three Calders.** *She and her younger brother, Sandy, who later became renowned for his mobile sculptures, were taught to read by their mother, an artist herself. They lived in the Southwest for a time during her childhood, while her father was recovering from tuberculosis, then moved to California in 1915 when he became sculptor-in-chief for the Panama Pacific International Exhibition.*

That same year she entered the University of California at Berkeley and met Kenneth Hayes, whom she married in 1916. Her husband's work took them to Washington state, and there, following her mother's example of teaching her and Sandy, she started her first school when her children were small. Later, in California, determined to avoid any war-affiliated industry, her husband began to manage the Puro Water Filtering Com-pany, and she helped considerably after he became ill. Then she started another school and workshop in the basement of her home, where hundreds of children learned to work with clay, linoleum cuts, looms, and other arts and crafts. The school prospered for eighteen years.

Always active in war resistance, the Hayeses worked before World War II with the Quaker Emergency Peace Campaign and vigorously resisted nuclear proliferation. She was widowed in 1966.

Peggy Hayes has devoted herself to many environmental and peace campaigns, as well as to the arts. She is also at work on a second book, which will concentrate on her brother's later work and life. She was one of the cofounders of the University of California Art Museum Council, and an endowment for awards for art students at the University of California was established in her name following a celebration of her eighty-eighth birthday.

TEAMPLAY

She laid her graduation dress out on the bed. It didn't look too bad—hadn't yellowed at all. The three-tiered skirt had ironed out crisply. The lace on the sleeves was as fresh and fragile as when it was first made and came down below her elbows almost as if it had been designed for her as she was now and not for a girl graduate. The dress was the emblem of the end of the first part of her life: Cal, class of 1917. She'd wear it tonight in celebration of the third part of her life. Whimsical, maybe, to wear her graduation dress to her eighty-eighth birthday party. But if people wanted to be whimsical enough to declare Margaret Calder Hayes Day, they had to expect she'd respond in kind.

"We'll do it as a fundraiser, Peggy," Bonnie Grossman had said on the phone, "for art students. You can't say no to that." Saying no was not her strong suit, except to nukes and developers.

She had agreed finally. "It'll be nice to give a leg up to the next Michelangelo."

She opened the drawer with the jewelry, trying to decide whether to wear a necklace she'd made herself or one of Sandy's. Of course, she could never have made anything herself without her brother, for she would never have thought of sitting down with wire and a pair of pliers. Sandy was the teammate of the first part of her life.

Gallia tres omnis divisa in partes est. That was how she felt about her life; like Caesar's Gaul, it was divided into three parts. The main trouble with this last part was no teammate, not a particular one anyhow. In the first part she'd had her brother, with his wildly playful imagination. How fortunate they were, innocently going on the assumption that all children had paints and clay to fiddle with. Poor as they were, Mother and Father had fostered their resourcefulness. And it had eventually paid off in Sandy's art.

Her personal payoff had started as far back as she could remember. As kids, she and Sandy went to the first Rose Bowl game, which had horse-drawn floats; they came home from the game and made horses out of broomsticks, with rope for manes and tails and rattles; they made chariots out of orange crates. It was always like that with Sandy. And, of course, Mother had made it possible, with her joyful, fun-loving nature, willingly giving time to her family, setting aside her own gifts as a painter.

The good humor in Sandy's work had come straight from Mother. Peggy smiled, remembering how she found out that everybody starts from the bottom in learning. She'd had the naive notion you took off from your parents' shoulders, that you were born with their knowledge and just added to it. Then when they were living in Arizona, watching a ranch hand break a young colt that had been born to a perfectly tame mare, suddenly it dawned on her that no matter how intelligent Mother and Father were to her and Sandy, they both had a lot to learn. It was the shock of her young life.

Still, what a terrific start they got. She thought of her mother in her later years, still carrying in her pockets those little scarlet crocheted balls she'd made with bells inside them in case a child came along in need of a little present. In the fifties, after Father's death, she had a studio. With more time she had hoped to paint, but she said her eyes were playing tricks on her. Disgusting—you have a palette and a brush, and you think you're putting paint on a canvas, but you're not touching it. It's that thing about focusing. How well Peggy understood it now.

Mother's life—she could see to the heart of it so clearly now, the gaiety she created for them out of her own self-denial. Father's life as an artist had meant a lot too because—well, only their parents could have waited so patiently and supportively for Sandy to come into his own as the third Alexander Calder. Other parents would have wondered if he weren't going to be a failed engineer forever.

The telephone rang. It had been ringing all morning. That was one of the debits of the third part of life. The day was half over by the time you finished with the phone, took the dog for a walk, and swallowed the pills that kept you going.

It was Maggie Gee with another detail about the party. She was calling from Livermore. There was a time when Peggy might not have been willing to let a friendship develop with someone working within shouting range of a nuclear plant. After all, she was one of the people who picket Livermore, and she would as long as it was there. If it outlived her, she'd haunt it. Maggie was telling her about the birthday cake—it was to have a Calder theme, a three-ring circus on top of it. Bonnie was making animals of marzipan: a dancing bear, a lion, an elephant, a ringmaster; and Ron and Myra Brocchini were creating an audience in a grandstand out of hundreds of gumdrops which would go around the cake. "There'll be three hundred people there," she said. "Everyone loves you, Peggy."

She loved Maggie's horselaugh, even if she was a physicist at Livermore. That was something on the plus side of the third part of her life—learning you can bend with the wind and still hang on to what you are, what you believe.

It was a lucky thing she had developed that skill—she'd lose half her friends and family if she hadn't. Not over the nuclear freeze but because of a more home-based issue: sex and the new attitudes toward it. She remembered parading for votes for women back in 1918—she and her friends thought men would come over to a single standard; instead, women went over to the double. Thanks to the Pill. Or curses to it, depending which way you bent. She still thought there was too much emphasis on the act of sex, without any realization that if something more enduring, like love, didn't develop, you're in the soup.

Of course, she'd been lucky in that herself and had had only one great love in her life, Kenneth, the teammate of the second part of her life. There had been so much harmony between them, they'd had to look outside their marriage for the variety of some conflict. Of course, they'd found plenty working for peace. They'd opened their house for so many meetings in that cause. There, in those heavenly hills, a whole community had grown up around them. In their brown shingle houses they were like an enclave of extended families, people who valued nature, art, ideas. At the New Year's Eve block parties, everybody over the age of two would come, and dance everything from the bunny hop to the samba. Boys were known to dance with their mothers without expiring.

When they first got the house, she had patterned a design of cut glass and stone in their walkway, with two dolphins, one red and the other very dark. Her hair was dark brown in those days and Kenneth's red. An image came to her of his rugby shirt that his classmates had put in a case with other treasures in the Campanile, the shirt with holes all over the chest, torn in some athletic tussle. The Class of '16 shirt was in the case with the words she had written about the heart attack he had while making a golden anniversary speech to his class: "There was something tremendous in going out in full sail, flags flying, in the service of something he felt so keenly about and a place he loved so."

"*. . . in partes tres.*" She sighed. The third part, learning to live alone. In some ways it was easier, but in most ways not nearly so nice for a team person. Yet she could always call up something funny. She remembered the boys in the kitchen repeating off-color stories told them by the milkman when he left the bottles by the door. And

Kenneth calling them on it, saying, "Boys, remember your mother was once a lady." She had no time for regrets or for dwelling on the past, except perhaps on this birthday. She had too much to do, with crusading for the freeze and against the waterfront development, and getting to the book inspired by Sandy's letters, and all the joy she took in such simple things, like cutting the dog's hair down in the garden the other day.

She slipped into her graduation dress and smoothed her hair in the mirror. Well, thank heaven she had recovered from that bump on her leg in the garage last week. That would have kept her from dancing, and tonight she wanted to dance. She'd be the first to arrive at The Good Table and the last to leave. She'd dance all night in her graduation dress. Wasn't that what they wanted, her friends, to see her accept what they offered, acknowledgment of the enduring verities, that friendships extend throughout a life, that loyalties are true, that life is good and rich as long as we have it? She was proof of all that, and they were her team now—she couldn't let them down.

She gathered up her notes for the tiny speech she said she'd make about the scholarship fund. She added an opening comment she knew would make them laugh: "This is the kind of thing that doesn't happen to most people until after they are dead."

Alice Lindberg Snyder

Born May 27, 1909

Alice Lindberg was raised in Wisconsin and went to college at the University of Wisconsin in Madison. There she met and married William Snyder, a plant pathologist who later joined the faculty at the University of California at Berkeley. They had three daughters, and Alice is now grandmother to six.

She became a close friend of Margaret Gardner (also in this volume), whose husband was chairman of the plant pathology department. Both widows, the two women often swim laps together in the campus pool.

For years Alice felt uncomfortable as a faculty wife; active sports and dancing were more to her taste. As a widow, she has found time for the inner child she suppressed during her marriage. She has a broad range of activity, as well as being very well read. She went to Florence recently on an art-history study trip and has plans to go river rafting with her grandson. Her dancing is a joy to all her friends.

FREEDOM

The tap shoes she wanted were in the window of the Children's Bootery, so she went inside and asked for them. The salesman raised his eyebrows but lifted her foot onto his metal measure, out of habit maybe. She told him her size, said it hadn't changed in sixty years. Nice that they measure the children's feet every time, she thought, but this was her second childhood, not her first. "You been dancing that long too?" the young man asked.

"Just started," she said. Had a talent for it too, but she didn't boast. Actually, she did dance as a child and had had a few more lessons lately. The shoes were a must now, especially since Edie's call.

"You'd better come on and visit now, Alice. You're going to get old. You're going to die like everybody else, so *do it now!*" By most standards she was ancient already. So *now* was the time.

All those things she hadn't done when Bill was alive she had begun to do now just because they were in her, the perfectly harmless things she had done as a young girl: sailing, swimming, whistling, tap-dancing. That fun-loving nature of her childhood hadn't died; she just hadn't turned it loose all those years. Now it was taking over. Let other people worry about brittle bones if they wanted to—that was their lookout. Or the impropriety of an old woman who sticks her fingers between her teeth to hail a cab. Let them think her a zany eccentric if they liked. She was through with neglecting the part of herself that wanted to play.

She was thinking of taking her grandson rafting on the Rogue River with a friend of his. Better not wait on that. And of going with Edie to the Hebrides to hear the wind shriek in their ears.

"Do you think it's unusual for someone my age to tap?" she asked the shoe salesman.

"Unusual but okay by me," the salesman grinned and tied the bow on the tap shoes for her. "How about a demonstration?"

"Move that stool aside," she said. "I'll show you something right here." Still sitting in her chair, she let her feet beat a quick rhythm on the vinyl floor and hummed "The Sidewalks of New York." The salesman was impressed. "You see, it'd be great therapy for somebody in a wheelchair. Anyone can learn to tap-dance."

The salesman wrapped up the shoes. "And I'll have one of those balloons you give away too, please," she said.

Alice was into taboo-busting. She wasn't going to sit back and be the widow of a university professor who limited herself to activity suitable to her years and status. She had poured at her last faculty tea. Now she was going to become all that she could be.

She was grateful that so much was available to her here in the Bay Area. After Bill's death, she had gone to Langley Porter Clinic to a support group designed by psychologists for widows. Her psychologist friend, Beth, had helped her too. Together they had reached into that ancient rage at her mother. Beth's question, "What is the worst thing that could happen to your mother?" brought an astonishing response: "Nothing could be bad enough." She hadn't realized how much resentment she was carrying with her into her advanced years. The experience was like catching hold of a whole gunny sack of jewels; so many insights followed. Even the hard scenes shone with

brilliance, illumination. She had found her way to giving up her resentments, toward both her mother and her husband. During most of their marriage, she had endured an internal struggle against his conservatism. When she remembered Bill now, it was for the times he made her laugh, not for the times she had to leave the room to protest his racial views. Now it was his humor and energy that she recalled with pleasure. "Grandma and Grandpa were making so much noise laughing and talking in the next room I couldn't sleep," granddaughter Megan had once complained.

Most important, perhaps, she lived now with the consciousness that what her friend Edie had said was true—she was going to die. She didn't know how or when, but she knew it. She figured that by the time you were eighty-two, you had a right to know death was coming up, that it might bring even further illumination.

Do it now. That had become a slogan popping into her mind. Her cousins met her plane at the Chicago airport. They drove past a black neighborhood, and one of them used the word *coons*. She couldn't believe her ears. Images from her marriage surged up. Bill sitting at the table with the newspaper, expounding. Now she had to do more than leave the room. Now she never let such a remark pass. She said, "I feel hurt when I hear something like that. I think of the black people I know and feel as if I've let someone spit in their faces." The cousins looked startled.

"One thing about getting old," she said to them. "is the freedom to say what I believe." And freedom wasn't complete without responsibility. The cousins looked ashamed, said they were sorry. Maybe they thought about it.

Edie found the tap shoes in her suitcase as she helped her unpack. "Tonight I'll take out the old 78's," she said.

She had invited a partner, a man well up into his eighties who had been an economics professor. But he could still dance. They gave Alice a hat and a cane. "Your legs are like a Rockette's," the old guy said.

He kept up with her pretty well, through all of "Tea for Two"; even if he didn't remember all the words, he had the music.

Julia Child

Born August 15, 1912

Unlike the woman to whom marriage brings the end of a career, Julia Child found her vocation after she and her new husband, Paul, moved to France, where he was cultural attaché for the State Department. After her first lunch in France, in Rouen, she was hooked. "I didn't know such food existed." On childhood visits to her grandmother's house in the Midwest, there were cakes in the oven and fresh vegetables on the table, wonderful chicken. But in those days haute cuisine had not ignited the middle-class consciousness; it remained for her in her middle years to light the flame.

After college (Smith, 1934), Julia McWilliams worked for a time in public relations and advertising, but soon an invalid mother drew her back home. When her mother died, she went to Washington, D.C., and during World War II worked in the Office of Strategic Services (OSS), which sent her to the China-Burma-India theater of war. There she and Paul Child met; he was an artist ten years her senior, "Eastern, very impressive, much more sophisticated than I—I felt awkward and hickish." They were married in 1946, when he was in the United States Information Agency. His diplomatic service lasted fifteen years, and it was while they were in France that her culinary career began.

She enrolled at the Cordon Bleu in 1950. "I was very lucky: They still had chefs with the fine old classical training, so I got all the fundamentals." She studied for about six months—"until they began to prepare dishes so fancy nobody could afford to make them." Classes were at 7:00 A.M., and they cooked until 11:00; then she rushed home to prepare lunch for Paul, back from the embassy for the long lunch period of the French.

Julia met Simone Beck, who introduced her to her friend Louisette Ber-

tholle, both dedicated cooks. The French women were writing a cookbook for the United States, and enlisted her, an American, to help them with it. The three women also started a cooking school—L'École des Trois Gourmandes—teaching Americans in France. Paul always helped at the dinners prepared by the students. During the next nine years, the women taught and wrote, perfecting their instructions for Americans.

When Julia and Paul returned to the states, it was with the manuscript that became **Mastering the Art of French Cooking,** published in 1961.

Public television had just replaced "educational" television and a station approached her to talk about cooking for a half-hour live show. She took along a hot plate and her copper bowl and whipped up an omelette; her television series "The French Chef" was born. It has established her firmly in the minds of millions of viewers as the greatest American authority on French cuisine.

Julia credits her success with factors beyond her control, to her good fortune to live in France after World War II, to the fact that the American palate began to develop and was further enhanced by cheap air travel, and to the presence of the Kennedys' French chef in the White House. "We were coming out of the war years and the frozen-food era."

Since then she has made appearances on the "Good Morning America" program and created another series, "Dinner at Julia's." She has prepared articles for **Parade Magazine** and made some video teaching cassettes of one-hour lessons. Her new book will be **Mastering the Art of Good Cooking.** Ever since she and Paul prepared the index together for the first book, Paul has worked with her in every project, a vital teammate.

MARRIAGE

Throughout Julia Child's career, her husband has played a large part. "He's the painter and photographer, involved in everything," she says—whether shelling peas for her "Good Morning America" appearances or cracking eggs for "The French Chef." ("It's such fun, we'd *pay* to do it.") Julia is always ready to credit her husband for his support.

"In the early days of TV, we had no help at all. Paul did dishes and peeled potatoes. Sometimes he is introduced as Mr. Julia Child, but I don't think he minds."

He says, "I don't do it for credit—I do it because we want to get on with our mutual life. Whatever needs to be done, we do it."

She describes him as a "resident poet and a one-man art factory" and understands the need for retreat that such work creates. "We're lucky. We decided to do things together as much as possible, not to go our separate directions. Even little things we do together, like washing dishes. We each need long solitary periods but can work in proximity."

"There is a difference between us," Paul says. "On the whole, Julie likes human beings—anybody."

"No, not anybody!"

"I'll start again. Julie likes almost everyone, responds to everyone. My outlook is different."

"I think Paul and I are good for each other. He keeps me down a little bit, and I push him up a bit. I'm the optimist and he's the pessimist."

That balance fosters their mutually shared career. They made plans for a midlife career change at a time when neither imagined it would be in the public eye. One day during their years of public service, Paul approached her with the plan. He said, "Julie, next Thursday I'm going to be half a hundred years old." She said, "So what?" He said, "This implies certain things. Let's say that we'll go on with our two lives for another ten years; then when I'm sixty and you're fifty, we'll leave the Foreign Service and retire to Cambridge." That sounded fine to Julia; they were tiring of the bureaucracy. "We thought we might open a little ice cream parlor or something of the sort," Julia said.

However, when Julia was fifty, their "retirement" moved into high gear for them both. Knopf decided to publish the book she wrote with Simone Beck and Louisette Bertholle. She and Paul toured the country teaching French cooking; soon the TV series "The French Chef" was under way, and many other projects followed. Nowadays they work in their apartment in Santa Barbara, where they spend winters, or in either of their two houses, Cambridge and southern France.

"We create our atmosphere wherever we are, just settle down and go to work. We really don't take vacations. We always say that wherever we are, *it's* at."

If happiness is the conviction that wherever you are is where the action is, she and Paul are not recluses. Much of their time is spent with people younger than they. "We're lucky to be with younger people a lot—they're the future. There are so many good careers in cooking, in restaurants, in writing about food. I'm very much interested in encouraging young people.

"Just the other day the *Parade* staff had come to work, and we realized that the people here represented five decades, from twenty to eighty." Once every few months the staff meets in her Cambridge house to prepare four articles. "From editor, to assistant cook, to dishwasher, to designer, to photographer (Paul)—the age spread is marvelous."

They are at work on a video project with Russ Morash, her producer for "The

French Chef" and "Dinner at Julia's." Morash's wife, Marian, is part of his team. They are making a series of one-hour lessons, each concentrating on a single aspect of cuisine—poultry, meat, soups, salads, pasta—which will be sold by Knopf in a new marketing program. Morash, now fifty, was much younger, of course, when he began to work with the Childs. Julia said, "An older friend of ours from the Foreign Service, Rose Manell, is the food designer. I don't really feel any difference in ages unless people just seem awfully old and creaky or awfully young and immature. I think it's the profession that brings us together, not the age group, and we learn from each other.

"We're lucky to be in the arts. It's wonderful to see people deeply enthusiastic about what they're doing. And then television is such fun!"

Even though their retirement has not turned out exactly as they planned, they are mindful that some ultimate retirement may become necessary. The unexpected changed their plans once; they wouldn't welcome it if they weren't together. "We've been very lucky," Julia says, although she admits to a terror of being left, of surviving her husband, as women have a tendency to do. But together they share a determination to maintain their health through moderation—even in food (although she acknowledges a love of martinis). And they are committed to a plan they have made should they be unable "to stay right in the mainstream. We don't kid ourselves." Acknowledging that helplessness may be a possible eventuality, the Childs have chosen a retirement residence for themselves. She feels that if the means are available, everyone should decide such things for themselves.

"It's the only responsible thing to do," Julia says, "to make sure that no relative has the burden of taking care of you when you go ga-ga, or of deciding where to put you." They have no children, but feel such decisions should not in any case be left as a problem for children. Wanting to feel some control over decisions about their final days, they have also made living wills.

"If you pretend old age is not going to happen, it will fall right on you. I think it is very selfish of people not to have planned ahead for the day they slip off the raft."

They have applied to a residence in Santa Barbara, one chosen by many of their friends, with whom they expect eventually to enjoy a late-life community. "We have all looked it over and put our names in. You have to be mentally adequate, and you have to walk in on your own two feet, although in this one there is no age limit. We have a very good lawyer who is committed to telling us when the time has come." Some other friends have decided to move into a place near their Virginia homes. "One friend was fortunate to get his wife in just before she began to go senile. Facing up to old age and choosing where you'll go can help you be at peace with yourself."

Meanwhile, they feel far from ready for the option they've made. "Painting and cooking—we'll never live long enough to learn the half of it," Julia says. "A passionate interest in what you do is the secret of enjoying life, perhaps the secret of long life, whether it is helping old people or children or making cheese or growing earthworms."

Stella Nicole Patri

Born November 1, 1896

Stella Patri first became interested in bookbinding when her former husband, Giocomo Patri, a well-known artist, was working on a book on linoleum cuts, illustrations for a story. In order to bind the book, she took lessons from Octavia Holden, then later, in 1938, she worked with another well-known woman, book-maker Peter (Edna) Fahay.

She was sixty-three when she started her own bookbinding business, about a decade after her divorce. Her three sons, all architects, each had two children. She wanted, she said, to assert some independence.

First she went to Rome in 1960, where she studied paper restoration for the Italian government, then to France for lessons in finishing, and to England to study book restoration. In 1966, at the time of the great flood in Florence, she was among the first volunteers for CRIA, the Committee to Rescue Italian Art in the Bibliotequa Nacionale.

She studied in Japan during a number of visits, so it was natural for her nephew to think of her when he wanted a traveling companion to accompany him to Japan.

BINDING

Stella said no when her nephew Maurice invited her to go to Japan with him. She could scarcely see and had a cataract operation scheduled. "Travel is too wearing for older people," she said, "I might get sick and be a perfect nuisance." He was a dear thoughtful nephew, and she was thankful he wanted to do this for her, but no, she couldn't go to Japan again. She knew it was for her sake he had dreamed up the idea.

He asked her to think it over. They could take things very slowly. They'd go in April before it was too hot. She could gather materials for that book she was doing.

"It's not a book," she said, "I don't even know why I'm doing it."

Maurice asked her to think it over. She could let him know later.

She heard one of the grandchildren run up the stairs to the apartment overhead. She smiled, remembering how her work had sprung partly out of her resistance to being a grandmother. About the time her sons were marrying, she told herself: I'm not the grandmotherly type. Nevertheless, the family had remained very close, even shared the same house, thanks to her attitude maybe. She loved her grandchildren, saw them often, but was no granny.

In her workroom she turned on the light. The bindery room, where she had spent so many years in meticulous work, seemed dark to her now, though she knew it was only her vision. Over the large box in which she had put her project, she clicked on another light.

She called it a scrapbook, something she had started when her sight failed her; she could do this even if she didn't get her full sight back. She had collected all the elements that go into Japanese paper. Years ago when she had first started binding books, she had grown to appreciate Japanese paper for its long fibers and its beauty. She wanted each page in the scrapbook to contain an example from Japanese book- and papermaking, things the Japanese draw from their environment—fibers, threads, rope, woven strips. They made papers woven of cotton and silk, dyed different colors, hand-rolled. It was such colorful, beautifully crafted work. She wanted the book to reflect the devotion to craft that always touched her, the caring that drew her into bookbinding in the first place. She was touched that Maurice had thought of traveling with her.

She hadn't always been so cautious about traveling. Not in her sixties and seventies. But at eighty-eight? In 1960 she had gone to the American cultural attaché in Rome. She was already divorced then and was having a visit with her husband's family, who were still her friends. She wanted to learn from the Italians—they were doing such interesting work in restoration—but they hadn't answered her letters offering herself as an apprentice. The attaché was able to arrange it: an apprenticeship to a woman repairing paper for the library.

Stella was sixty-four, and her only income was Social Security. Ninety dollars a month. You couldn't do a whole lot of lounging around the Via Veneto on that. She led the austere life of a lonely foreign student. A dollar for her room, a dollar for food, and a dollar for carfare. It was not the romantic episode it sounded. In the same financial crunch she went on to work with specialists in Paris and in London.

That had given her the confidence to open her own business when she got back to San Francisco. Slow at first, the business drew mostly Bibles. Old family relics, usually of only sentimental value, the large Bibles with family records in the center, shabbily bound and printed on newspaper and sold door to door years ago. She'd try to explain to the people about rare books, which were indeed sometimes Bibles, try to persuade them to let her remove the family record and bind those nicely. But, no, they usually insisted she work on the whole book. Then at last Mrs. Tomasini at the San Francisco Medical Library gave her a chance—fourteen medical books at once. It was a risky move on her part, Stella thought. She should have sent just one to try her out. Fourteen books. That set her up. She was as busy as she wanted to be after that.

The next trip to Italy was such a contrast to the first. She was not lonely, there wasn't a moment for it. She was in London when word came of the disaster in Florence. The Bibliotequa Nacionale had flooded; the entire first floor was so weighted with water that it crashed into the basement. Every book was water damaged. All the bookbinders she knew in England were volunteering to help. She went too.

The Italians were well organized. They turned the main reading room into a restoration workroom: special stainless steel sinks, floating beds, netting trays for separating the pages. Each book had an index card on which the damage was noted, and the repair. She dug in, helping the young Italian volunteers, many of whom had never even owned a book. They worked hard, having an innate appreciation for these ancient treasures. She stayed a month, then went home to her business. And they called her back. They offered her a job teaching a new set of volunteers. Almost immediately she was on another plane.

It had been wonderful to stay busy all these years. She was grateful that she had begun this late-life career. To make something last, or come back to life, something rare and beautiful—that was worth any amount of trouble.

Impulsively she reached for the phone and dialed her eye doctor's number. The nurse said, sure, she could postpone the operation until the summer months. A trip sounded like a great idea if she felt well enough. Then she called her nephew. "Maurice, it sounds too good to miss," she said. "I'll go with you."

Inez Marks Lowdermilk

Born January 26, 1890

Inez Marks was born in Wasco, Oregon, and grew up near San Bernardino, California. After finishing her master's degree at the University of Southern California, she applied to the Methodist Board, which she says was the nearest thing in those days to the Peace Corps, and in 1916 she accepted a five-year assignment to Szechwan Province. She traveled more than 3,000 miles in China at a time when roads were slabs of stone, like those reported by Marco Polo. She started fifteen schools for girls, trained twenty-six teachers, and persuaded more than two hundred women to unbind the feet of their daughters.

She and Walter Lowdermilk were married in 1922. He had served in World War I in France and afterward worked on the Hoover Commission for Belgian Relief. After their marriage, they went to China to work in the famine prevention program in Nanking. Throughout the rest of their married life, during which they had two children, a son and a daughter, they devoted themselves to programs of world scope in soil conservation. They became dedicated to the Jewish cause in Palestine before World War II, and for years Inez made appearances throughout the United States to raise money for Jewish rescue and rehabilitation. Walter's book, **Palestine, Land of Promise,** *was widely influential. In 1951 they lived in Israel, where Walter worked as a volunteer in soil restoration.*

In the decade since her husband's death, she has shared her home with Chinese students.

TENDER MERCY

I would prop my hymnal card up on the dashboard of the car before I took off. It had the first lines of twenty-five hymns, and they reminded me of the words. Every week I went to visit my husband in the hospital and would sing all the way, an hour's drive. I missed only twice, once when I was about eighty-four and was sick myself. What happened with Walter and I was like the wonderful one-horse shay; everything was just fine, then everything went to pieces. While I was recovering from my operation, a friend drove me to see Walter. I had to miss visiting him again when I went to Israel to attend a tribute to him that the president of Israel gave at his home to commemorate all that Walter had done to help the Jewish pioneers restore the worn-out soil in the Holy Land.

I was fortunate to have an air-conditioned car, so I would roll up the window, and once I got headed toward the San Mateo Bridge, I would begin to sing loudly all the way to the Veteran's Hospital near Stanford. "Trust and Obey" and "A Mighty Fortress Is Our Lord" and "Brighten the Corner" and "Blessed Assurance, Jesus Is Mine." Twenty-five hymns would take one hour. Instead of arriving depressed like some of the other wives I saw there, I arrived in good spirits. I loved the hymns.

All the way my Saviour leads me
What have I to ask beside?
Can I doubt his tender mercy
Who all my life has been my guide . . .

I was always the more religious one, although Walter used to come and sit beside me in the little church in Wilcox. In those days I didn't know I had much voice, but he said later he came because he liked to hear me sing.

When we were growing up, Walter's people lived on one side of the valley, and we were on the other. He was president of the student body, editor of the *Wildcats*, a tennis champ, and was about to go to Oxford as a Rhodes scholar. I was just a pathetic eighteen-year-old girl. There seemed to be no future for me. I was a high school dropout and was going nowhere. So, to me, Walter was up on a pedestal, and I never imagined he'd consider me. On Sundays he'd ride horseback behind our carriage and come to our house. Because there was no place else to go, I thought.

I was so desperate and lonely in those days, I decided to pray. I prayed to the Lord to guide me and make me useful. Within a few minutes I knew I was going back to school. Eventually I got a scholarship in voice and became the soloist in the university women's glee club. I worked my way through school, then asked for more guidance. The next thing I knew the Methodist Board had agreed to send me to teach in China.

In China the people loved seeing my big feet, the kind of clothing I wore, and so on. An intriguing thing—here was this tall white girl with big feet, and I could talk so that they could understand me. As we went from village to village, I would walk a lot because I didn't like them to have to carry my sedan chair on those mountain trails. The only wheeled vehicle in those days was the wheelbarrow. Nothing on land moved faster than a water buffalo.

My chair bearers just knew I would be robbed by bandits and were afraid. We were stopped by bandits, all right. They knew I was carrying a lot of money because of the weight of the chair. I kidded the bandits—pretending they were sheriffs—and told them I was grateful for a safe passage, thanks to them. I think they let me pass because I was such a novelty.

Whenever I would open a school, mothers would come to me and say they could get a much finer husband for their daughters if they had an education, and so a few enrolled. Those who attended school had more prestige, so then others came. I would tell them that if education gave them a better husband, they wouldn't have to bind their feet to attract one. I reasoned and pleaded with them.

They would start the binding even before the first grade. They would take the child's four toes and fold them under and under and under, a little more each day until they made nests for themselves in the bottom of the foot. And the child could never put down her foot, so she would try to play and run on her heels. It was just tragic. The little things would run like that after me on the street. When they were eight or nine, their mothers would begin to work on the great toe.

I was always interested in how women are treated everywhere. Confucius said, "Woman is a human being but of a lower order than man." And a Moslem writer, "Woman is the toy with which man plays; in him is light and understanding, in her is darkness."

When I was coming back from the East to visit my parents in Pasadena, my train stopped to put on coal in Missoula, Montana, and I happened to know that Walter was there. It was a beautiful day. People came down to the train to get the Kansas City newspaper, and I imagined he was in the crowd. I bought a penny postcard and wrote him that I'd passed through and remembered him. I didn't ask him any questions or tell him anything about me, and when I got back, a letter came quite soon in which he said he hadn't seen his mother at Christmas for three or four years and he would have to stop by Pasadena to see me and the Rose Parade. He was better looking than I remembered and very much the Oxford gentleman. Forty-eight hours later he proposed.

Walter was called in by Franklin Roosevelt to start the Soil Conservation Service, and even after he retired, he went wherever he was asked to help out.

We happened to be in Swaziland on my sixtieth birthday. Walter was retired then, but he was anxious to help in the emerging African countries. I always went along as part of his team and would help with his writing. I took his notes on four continents, in twenty-eight countries. In Swaziland they had so many cows. The land was terribly overgrazed. No cow was ever used for milk or butter or meat. A lovely Swazi gentleman was taking us around, and I wanted to know how many cows a woman would be worth, so I asked him how many I was worth at sixty. He looked very embarrassed and refused to answer. I persisted, and finally he said, "Madam, at your age you would not be worth even one cow; you would perhaps be worth two goats." Well, I've lived another thirty years since then, so now I must be worth no more than a scrambled egg or two.

My church has formed the Inez Marks Club to support my schools in China. My daughter, Wester, saw the schools only last year. Her husband was invited to give a series of lectures, and she let the Chinese know that her mother had opened some schools in Szechwan, so they invited her too. The teachers got together and had a lovely dinner for her. She found that the first kindergarten in all of western China, which I opened, was still there. Of course, the revolution took them over and changed everything, all of China. I used to say it'd take a century to do away with footbinding, and it was done away with in a year or two.

People could do that with the bomb if they wanted. You can do away with any evil. So much has been accomplished already—no more slavery. It's a matter of believing it is possible to stop making bombs. Like footbinding, we could just stop doing it.

Chica stayed with me for two years, longer than any of the other students from China, who usually are allowed to stay only for a month or so. She never saw bound feet. I know more of the history of their country than these students do, and of womanhood in the past.

I try never to proselytize. Chica used to read the little woodblocks I have around the house with aphorisms on them: "I'd rather attempt to do something great and fail than attempt to do nothing and succeed," and "There is no gain without pain" and so on. She said they helped her English. But she wouldn't read the ones that included God. Yet after she left here, she wrote, "I hope God will continue to bless you, because you have been such a blessing to me."

Of course, the Chinese still respect elders, and they fuss over me, carry out the trash. If they see I've been working hard, they insist on bringing a bowl of hot tea or soup. They take over the cooking of fresh vegetables because they know I don't like to cook them. Chica and some of the other girls and I did exercises together. It always astonished them that I could kick higher than they and can touch the floor without bending my knees. "How can you do that?" they'd say. I'd say, "Well, if you just want to do a thing, why, you'll do it."

After Walter died, the school started sending me the Chinese students. They knew how interested I am. I remain interested in everything, especially Walter's work. He was such a prophet of the way things were going on this earth. He said, "Civilization is running a race with famine, and the outcome is in doubt."

We shared a very lovely old age. He would rise early to work in his garden, and at eight o'clock sharp he'd bring me coffee with a fresh blossom on the saucer.

During the last five years, after his stroke, when he was in the hospital, the hymns saved my spirits. It was a lonely thing, to go down there; you can imagine how lonely it was to me. There are so many mental cases down there that they have all the patients locked up. I would have to wait until they unlocked him and let him come out to visit with me. Then it was sad to have him locked up again. I would always say a prayer on the way to the freeway for guidance for a safe journey home. In the car I would sing "Count Your Blessings." You know how it ends: "It will surprise you what the Lord has done."

Ursula Hodge Casper

Born December 13, 1907

In her seventies Ursula Casper published a book that distilled a life-long study of body movement, Joy and Comfort Through Stretching and Relaxing. *Practical and inspiring, it offers suggestions for exercise to those who cannot move vigorously and who may not be ambulatory:*

Ursula grew up on an orange ranch in Redlands, California. In 1928 she opened an exercise studio in San Francisco. Shortly thereafter she was married, and in 1936 her only child, Rao, was born.

During World War II, she worked with migrant farm workers for the Farm Security Administration and was personnel supervisor at the U.S. Naval Drydocks in Hunters Point, San Francisco. Around 1947, when two obstetricians hired her to help teach techniques in muscular relaxation to expectant mothers, she began the work that has occupied her ever since. She has taught dancing, posture, muscular relaxation, and meditation in many classes throughout the San Francisco area, for people of all ages, from brain-damaged children to elders in retirement homes.

In 1960 she married Harold Casper, who died in 1967.

She is often called upon to bring her knowledge of the body to public celebrations, such as the one described in her story.

BODY WISDOM

The theater at the Palace of Fine Arts was jammed with devotees of new-age psychology, and Ursula stood in the wings in her flowing gray robes and her Birkenstock sandals, wondering how she had gotten into this. She didn't think of herself as the Wise Old Woman–Underworld Figure she was supposed to represent. And she wasn't altogether confident of the degree–bona fide "movement specialist" who was putting the dance part of the program together. "We'll improvise," the young woman had said, "just get ourselves relaxed and centered—and go. Woman in three stages. *You* know."

The young woman was Woman-Stage-Center—young, touched by Venus, blessed by the Madonna maybe, with Demeter rolled up in there somewhere. A sweet little girl was playing a kind of Divine Child–Persephone and seemed all right, eight or nine years old. But Ursula wasn't so sure about herself. What did a Wise Old Woman *do* once she was centered? The movement specialist had suggested that at least she could take off her Birkenstocks, but this floor was so blasted cold.

The music started up, and the Woman-Stage-Center sent the child forth, in her pastel spring garments. Were those rose petals in her hands that she was scattering as she twirled? An unabashed steal from Isadora. Come on, she told herself, no judgment. Let go and relax. After all, if you don't fit the Wise part, you do fit the Old, seventy-five.

Relaxation had been her ally for decades now, had helped her re-create her life over and over again. Krishnamurti had said, "Die at the end of every day." He meant: Let go of everything; die each day so that the next morning will be fresh and new. It was a lesson she had spent some time cultivating. You might understand it right away, but you couldn't expect it to stay with you unless you worked at it.

Ursula had reason to work at it. Pregnant with her daughter, Rao, in the mid-thirties, she began to suffer from some unusual symptoms: extreme exhaustion and a magenta rash that covered her cheeks in a butterfly pattern. After some tests, her doctor told her that she must expect death from lupus at an early age. He told her to rest in bed, and, there, too tired to read, she began to explore every muscle of her body.

She had taught herself to bring her own organism under her mind's control, to relax its every inch completely. She was working for the life of her child as well as for her own. Flat on her back, she devised a system of subtle muscular movements that helped her to heal. She had always danced, and that gave her some knowledge of how the body worked, but never before had she explored it in such detail. She found that with careful concentration she could release the muscles of her lower back as never before—from the last lumbar vertebra to the muscles surrounding her anus—and experience a profound feeling of relief. All through her pregnancy she worked with her body in this way; and when Rao was born, her pelvis released the baby easily, even before the doctor could get to the hospital.

She had lived, ever since, prepared to die with every day, to let go. The lesson became part of her. Even when she forgot it—when Rao's father left her and she was ill again and had no money and felt such panic—even then the lesson came back to her, like a friend tapping her shoulder. Let go. As soon as she did, things moved for her; a way of reinventing her life presented itself. Slowly she taught herself what Alan Watts called the "wisdom of insecurity."

And eventually she had found Dr. William Kuzell, who worked with her and understood how she was trying to build up her own immune system through relaxation, and who gave her the drug she knew her body would accept. She had not died at an early age at all. Here she was a Wise Old Woman. But it had taken work every day. And there had been some recurrences.

Her life had filled up with the rewards that had come as a result of that philosophy —friendships with so many wonderful students over the years. Even Harold.

She smiled, remembering how he became her student after they were married. Harold was sixty-five when one of her students introduced him to her. He had had a stroke, was gentle, cautious. After they were married, she knew better than to offer the relaxation to him, unless he asked for it. But one day when she was holding a class at home, she opened the door unexpectedly; there was Harold, following her directions on the other side of the door. He hadn't wanted to ask to join the class but knew he needed the work.

After that he had helped her find a senior center in the Mission that would let them bring movement classes to older people. That was in the sixties, before the world woke up to the fact that older people need exercise more than the young. Many other centers had refused them—"You can't move people around like that; they'll drop dead." Or maybe just let go, Ursula thought.

The dance was progressing; the young girl's petals were blowing across the stage. She and Woman-Stage-Center were dancing together, whirling about one another. Finally the young woman nodded toward Ursula, as if to say we're waiting for you. They'd run out of fancy stuff maybe. Anyhow, Ursula was relaxed. She kicked out of her Birkenstocks and went on stage. She didn't join them at once. She moved upstage, a background presence. Crone, shade from the underground, gray eminence, or Minerva—she swayed slowly, lifted her arms in a half-menace, half-invitation. She relaxed. Something would happen.

Something had happened after Harold's death, another letting go. They had had such fine years, more than seven. She knew she had to reinvent her life again And there was her sister, Mary, widowed now and needing help, and her brother, Ben. It was logical for the three of them to try to renew their family in their old age. Ursula's house had room—she could manage to have them there. She could always find space for herself, could go up above the walkway with the pink hawthorn, where the ground was carpeted with sorrel, to a flat spot carved out of the hill. There she could lie on the ground below the redwoods and gaze at the sky. She could have the hour alone that she needed every day to find the new transition.

The Divine Child–Persephone came up to her, reached up and so did Woman-Stage-Center, both making an appeal in movement. And so she joined them, and they whirled in a spiral of birth, death, and rebirth. Then Ursula made a gesture to include the audience. She extended her arms to them, and many people came on the stage. As the music continued, everyone danced together.

The audience burst into tumultuous applause; some people were even crying, to Ursula's surprise. One of the women who had been dancing with them said to her, "When you came on, I don't know why, but I started to weep."

She was smiling though; at least it wasn't a complaint. She probably just needed to let go.

Ruth Bernhard

Born October 14, 1905

I shall die young, at whatever age the experience occurs.

—R.B.

The attitude of seeing everything that happens to her, even death, as "experience" has kept Ruth Bernhard young and attentive to the possibilities in every moment of life. She was born in Berlin, the only child of parents who were divorced in her infancy. She saw her mother twice after that, only long enough to observe her "terrific sense of style." Her father was an artist, about to become a successful designer in advertising, a young business in those days, and he placed his child in the care of two sisters, Helene and Katarina Lotz, who were teachers. At eleven she went to boarding school and later attended the Academy of Fine Arts in Berlin. Both her father and mother remarried, and eventually she had a sister and three brothers, with whom she formed close ties. But she credits the Lotz sisters, who taught her to read at four, with encouraging her curiosity and delight in life, which were the foundation of her artistic work.

In 1927, at her father's suggestion, she moved to New York, where he had been working for some years. A magazine hired her as a photographer, but she found the tasks too impersonal. She bought a friend's 8-by-10 camera and began to photograph the work of her father's associates—designers, sculptors, potters, weavers. Then in 1934 she became the photographer for Machine Age, *published by the Museum of Modern Art.*

She says she did not take her work seriously until 1935, when, while vacationing on a beach in Southern California, she met Edward Weston by chance and saw his work. The following year she moved to Southern California with the expectation of studying with Weston, but he had in the meanwhile moved north to Carmel. She remained in Los Angeles to work but acknowledges her debt to Weston, who had a very strong influence on her.

She moved to San Francisco in 1953 and has since made a small Victorian house her studio and home. In recent years she has become widely acclaimed, and her work is in permanent collections worldwide. She has taught numerous workshops on campuses in the United States and abroad. A monograph of her work, "Collecting Light," has been published, as have been two portfolios, "The Gift of the Commonplace" and "Eternal Body." A retrospective book of her work is in process.

Traveling last year in Japan gave her a new ambition—to climb Mount Fuji to celebrate her eightieth birthday.

LIGHT

The doorknob caught her attention at once. It was glowing with extraordinary light. That morning she had awakened later than usual for some reason. The light told her it was late, slanting into the room from the hallway window and striking the door as she hadn't seen it before, the glass doorknob in particular. Beautiful, she thought. She wanted to capture the glowing effect created by that particular slant of light.

She watched the doorknob, knowing that in moments the light would change. She would photograph it tomorrow, she told herself, and made a note to have everything ready at the same time. She checked her clock—exactly eleven.

Light had always fascinated her. Even in her childhood she had watched what it did to things, its effect upon the many creatures in the house: how it awakened the canaries, how it made the eyes of her guinea pigs gleam, the sheen it created on the white fur of her rabbits, and the way it brought the salamander to life, pulsing among the pebbles she and her guardians had picked up along their walks.

She loved the two sisters and their mother who became her family; their kind and loving care and encouragement helped her learn to be responsible for the menagerie she had accumulated. She was aware even now of the profound influence they had had upon her life. Their care had far exceeded the conscientious fulfillment of the charge her father gave them. They took her on nature walks, to the meadows, to the seashore; they indulged her enjoyment in collecting things, as if they knew she had eyes that especially needed to linger upon objects, as if they understood then what she had realized fully only in maturity: that her enjoyment of life began with her eyes. They would talk, these cultivated women, answering her many questions and encouraging her endless curiosity.

Since those days, she had always looked at everything as if for the first time. She had walked in her neighborhood for the past thirty years, always seeing everything with fresh eyes. She knew the condition of each tree, how the roots were behaving, the leaves, and each day she discovered something exciting. It was the same everywhere she went; that sense of seeing for the first time was always with her. The world had remained fresh and new to her for nearly eight decades.

Her photographs distilled her passion for life. A vision would come to her like a gift, pushing itself into her consciousness. A powerful feeling would come over her, telling her that she must capture the image that had caught her imagination. Often she would work for days to align the photograph with the spirit of that original impulse. It might be a seashell or a crushed teapot, a doll's head or a nude; but, whatever the subject, the image would come fully into her mind first, before it could appear on film and paper.

Because of the exciting light, a strong image was forming in her mind. She set her clock for a few minutes before eleven the next day, to remind herself to take her camera into the bedroom to capture the spirit of the doorknob.

The next morning, long before eleven, she knew she wouldn't get the picture. It was foggy and stayed that way for days.

Finally the sun came out, but no matter how she moved the door, the light never struck the glass quite as it had before. By now the sidereal movement of the heavens had left the doorknob with its everyday look. The magical moment had come and gone.

Then she thought, I can wait. She reached for her calendar and marked May 11,

the day she had first seen the astonishing light, a reminder to herself. Next year she would see if it came back. The miracle would surely happen again.

On May 11 a year later she awoke early to a sunny day. All morning her excitement grew. She prepared her camera. She knew there could be only one exposure. When the light came, she must be ready. The window in the hallway, the slant of the door— everything was as it had been the first time.

Watching for light was her vocation. Light and life were one and the same thing. There would be no life without light; it was the beginning; it was the substance that made things visible, that brought humanity to an awareness of what cannot be seen. It could enhance a thing and make it holy. This she had felt in her life as in her work, a sense of reaching for harmony beyond the human experience through light itself.

And here again this doorknob evoked that longing in her. It was only moments now before eleven o'clock. She lifted her camera.

The moment ticked past, and there it was, like a sunrise. The light moved to align the object before her with the spirit of her impulse, with the same gleaming reflections she had held in her mind for a year.

She clicked the shutter.

Monika Kehoe

Born September 11, 1909

Born in Dayton, Ohio, Monika Kehoe lived as a young child in Toledo, then moved to Fort Wayne, Indiana, when she was eight with her newly divorced mother. After Monika completed a convent schooling, her mother opposed her going to college because she was afraid of being left alone. Striking out on her own, Monika made her way. Through jobs and fellowships, she earned her doctorate from Ohio State University at the age of twenty-five in 1935. She was ready then for the career that has taken her all over the world. She began teaching at Mundelein College in Chicago. From there she went to Mills College in California, and through the next three-and-a-half decades she worked as an educator in Korea, Japan, Australia, and Ethiopia and held professorships at both McGill and the University of Montreal in Canada. She served the United Nations at its inception as staff counselor for the Secretariat and eventually retired as a professor from the University of Guam in 1977.

Retirement merely brought more varied activity into her life. In 1980 she worked as editor in a project supported by federal funds and the American Behavioral Research Corporation, the result of which was A Handbook for Women Scholars. *After that, from the campus of San Francisco State University, she continued her nationwide, pioneering studies of the lifestyles of lesbians over sixty-five years of age. Results of her first study of this special population have been reported at a number of gerontological and other scientific conferences. She is presently editing the lesbian issue of* The Journal of Homosexuality *in which her findings will appear. A second, broader study of lesbians sixty and over, made in 1984, received its principal funding from the Chicago Resource Center. She is planning further research, a comparison between gays and heterosexuals in late life based on the hypothesis that lesbians are necessarily survivors and may adjust better to aging than their nongay comtemporaries.*

Segments from Dr. Kehoe's memoirs, The Making of a Deviant: A Model for Androgyny, *have been published recently in* The Lesbian Path *(under two pseudonyms, Helen Trent and Isabel McTeigue) and in* New Lesbian Writings *(under her own name). The entire manuscript will soon be available in print. During her university career, Dr. Kehoe contributed to many books and published numerous articles in academic journals. She coauthored* The Laurel and the Poppy *(1968), a biographical novel on the poet Francis Thompson, and was editor of* Applied Linguistics: A Survey for Language Teachers *(1968).*

THE COMPANY OF WOMEN

The woman called early in the morning—well, it was later where she was calling from. Monika saw a Midwest plain, imagined the woman completely isolated in it, with nothing but a telephone and a long wire stretching across the emptiness.

After her first response, "Yes, I'm directing the study. Just two of us working on it really. Why? Well, we're interested in the most invisible minority, women over sixty-five who are lesbians."

The voice hesitated. "The flyer in my bookstore said something about 'emotional preference for women.' I wondered what that meant." Monika heard an appeal in this.

She had just come in from her half-hour morning run, poured herself a cup of coffee, and lighted the fire in her woodstove. In a few minutes she would be getting the room ready upstairs for her new housemate. But now she could take some time, especially given the lonely territory she sensed around this voice.

She sank into her chair with the coffee cup, gazing out on the clusters of fog on her hilltop in Bernal Heights. She said, "Actually, the flyer said 'emotional and/or sexual preference.' That wasn't an escape clause. We're interested in relationships, not only sexual activity."

Personally, she liked being associated with androgyny, had given a number of papers on that idea of maintaining an equipoise of the best of both sexes. However, she did not deny being deviant. In all areas of life.

"In anything you can think of, I'm deviant," she'd said to a colleague the other day. A jock all her life. Literally. Trained the Japanese horses that won in dressage in Helsinki in '56, tennis champ in '29, springboard diving champ, and on and on. Didn't know how to cook. Did none of the things most women do—was *willing*, just no good at them. She was born prematurely, kept herself fit all her life, wore the same size clothes now at seventy-five that she wore at eighteen, size eight. Same style too—most mornings, sweats and running shoes. She was different, all right. There'd been no passages in her life, no marriage, no motherhood, none of the usual age monitors. She never went through a decisionmaking process about being a lesbian. In fact, because she'd been so active, she'd almost never menstruated. That was a consequence known then among some athletes, becoming common knowledge only recently as young women train so fiercely nowadays for the Olympics.

The woman on the other end of the phone said, "I'm wondering about you. I mean, why are you interested in these older women?" Monika wondered about *her* anxiety. "I mean, are you working for the government?" Ah, that was it. A spy in the house of love?

Monika sipped her coffee. "Well, first off, I'm one of them. I'm seventy-five, very high on old age, and I'm a lesbian.

"This is not a witch hunt," Monika said with an edge of humor. "In fact, we're sending our questionnaires only to women who write to us asking for them. Or call." That might encourage her to take part, Monika thought. "As for my personal interest," she told the woman, "I figure there are more of us than people imagine. Statistics say 10 percent of the population is nonheterosexual. We've got sixteen-and-a-half million women over sixty-five in the United States—that's more than a million-and-a-half lesbians over sixty-five we never hear anything about."

There was a pause. Finally the woman burst out with several questions all at once: "Who's going to read the results? Does the questionnaire ask for intimate details? And

what do you think about women who leave their children, you know, to go live with another woman? I mean, are you encouraging that? You know, you see movies, all these new lifestyles—why are you doing this anyhow? What's behind it?"

Monika waited a moment. What to answer first? "Actually, my goal is to encourage a retirement community sympathetic to the lesbian mode. I suspect older lesbians are afraid of nursing homes that might not be sympathetic to their life histories. And as for women who leave their children—personally I don't care for that particular plot."

The woman drew a deep sigh. "Bless you," she said. Then the anxiety arose again. She said, "I'm still working. They know I'm over sixty-five, but they don't know the rest." She seemed unable to say lesbian. "I mean, would I be able to answer anonymously?"

Monika thought, well, it's a start. She said, "Out here we're more fortunate than women in other parts of the country."

No sooner had she spoken than she remembered herself in the late thirties at her early job at Mills College. She'd taught there for four years. She'd even built a house, much like this one, had been ready to stay there in the Oakland hills for good. But they didn't renew her contract. Nothing was ever said to her about why, but she knew it had something to do with her affectional preference. She had been devastated. Of course, she knew things had changed on that campus. So much had happened to her since then that the whole experience had no charge now, not even in memory. That was how things used to be.

In fact, she was grateful for the way things had gone. It was so comfortable in that small elitist college she might have stayed there forever, might never have gone to teach on Guam or in Australia. Might never have met the woman she had lived with for the eighteen years before her death. So much of her life had come about because of that single ostracism, so many good things. They had lived together throughout the world, had taught together on two continents. Thanks to Mills College and the way things used to be!

The woman on the phone had begun to talk now, really open up. "There are lots of us here," she said. "We all know about one another, but we don't let on. What I mean is, you give me courage. Send me a few copies of your questionnaire. I'll talk to them, show it to them, get them to take part. We're all so isolated."

Monika said, "I don't see why people don't get together. It doesn't have to be a physical relationship, but it can be emotionally very satisfactory. It's not healthy for older people to live alone." She took the address, reminded the woman she was running up her phone bill, and thanked her for the call. She wanted to get the house ready because Ruth would be moving in this afternoon. Ruth, a friend and contemporary, not a lover, shared her conviction that older people should not live alone but should share their lives.

The woman held on for one more question. "Dr. Kehoe, do you think I sound too secretive? I hope you understand."

How could she tell her that freeing oneself was always an individual matter? One thing she was sure of: you are never too old to take steps toward freedom. She said, "You're making the right step, talking to your friends, coming out with it. If it doesn't open them up, I'll be surprised."

Marie LeMarquand Lovejoy

Born May 8, 1901

Service in both the spiritual and social sense characterizes the life of Marie Lovejoy. For thirty-five years she was a social service worker for the Family Service Bureau of the New York Correctional Association. After World War II, she went to work for American Aid to France, where she was director of rehabilitation in Normandy. That work was a painful homecoming for Marie, who had been born in Paris. Although the family immigrated to the United States shortly after she and her twin brother, Louis, were born, her parents kept their heritage alive, and she grew up speaking French.

When they were thirteen, Marie and Louis took a trolley in Minneapolis to hear a speaker she had read about in the newspaper. His name was Krishnamurti. After his lecture, he greeted them and accepted them as members of the Theosophist Society, in which she has been active all her life.

Since she retired from her job as director of the Family Service Bureau, Marie has contributed generously of both time and money to the Theosophist Society. She worked for some years as a translator and assistant to the lecturer and author Geoffrey Hodson and financed the publication of several of his books.

Her own book, International Vegetarian Cuisine, *was published in 1978. For more than fifteen years she has led a meditation study group in her home. She is an active member of The Meditation Mount in Ojai, California, which studies the work of Alice Bailey.*

SPIRIT

And by came an Angel who had a bright key . . .
—William Blake
from *Songs of Innocence*

I was extremely tired; yet I faced an enormous task. The last two nights had been stressful and sleepless, and as I sat in the library with papers spread about me on the floor, I wondered how I would ever accomplish what I must do in one evening.

The opportunity to work for an extraordinary teacher had arisen late in my life. I was sixty-eight and had been retired for several years when I met Geoffrey Hodson and he asked me to translate into French for him during a conference in Geneva. There I shared a little house with Mr. Schmidt, the German translator. The next day, at the last meeting of the conference, our teacher needed a set of lectures for each of the students.

For the last two nights I had been up nursing Mr. Schmidt, who had had a stroke several days earlier. I took only occasional rests on the library sofa. Mr. Schmidt seemed to be recovering, but, of course, his translation task was far from complete. I would have to patch out his version of the lectures from my own skimpy German.

In the library rays of light from a streetlamp filtered through the high window, splashing shadows of the garden's large tree onto the papers on the library carpet. This was the last in the series of Mr. Hodson's lectures, the English, the French, and the German versions. There was still so much to do, and now I must finish it alone.

I didn't want to ask our teacher for help. He may have been able to find another translator, but he was very occupied with the lectures and dealing with many students. We were studying the effect of sound vibration upon matter, the link between the earthly plane and the unseen world that music offers, and the power of a single word. It was up to me to do the task I was assigned. The first rule of obedience goes at least as far back as the *Bhagavad-Gita*, teaching that the gift of understanding comes through unquestioning service. I had to cope with it somehow, rather than complain about the situation.

To do good by stealth—that was the ideal I had always tried to follow. For example, years ago my husband didn't know that I had arranged his meeting with the great teacher of the occult, Alice Bailey. He was an attorney and had been disabled by an accident in which a trolley completely crushed him. I had heard that Alice Bailey needed help with Greek and Latin for her writings, and I thought my husband could benefit from working with her, that she had the power to restore his faith in life. After meeting with her, he said to me, "She has a Tibetan guide who told her that I could help her." She had told him things about himself that she had no ordinary way of knowing. I said, "Work with her. You'll help to raise the human race." And so he worked as a volunteer for her Arcane Society for twenty-five years before he died. I told him, "I'll support the family," for his daughter had come to live with us.

It was the depth of the Depression, but with divine help I found a job in the welfare department in New York City. I worked for hospital and prison reform. When my sister was in Rockland Hospital, I went to a *PM* reporter to urge him to conduct an investigation that eventually exposed Rockland's snakepit. As case after case of human distress came into my office, I felt myself fortunate and humbled. My husband had good work to do, and so did I.

I have always believed that the invisible world is never very far away, even though I worked in that cruelest of everyday worlds. After World War II, I went back to Normandy to help in the little town where my father was born, Cruton. Devastation everywhere. I organized a household for young women from sixteen through twenty-five whose relatives had been killed. Two walls had been bombed out of the house, and the rain came through every day that winter. There was no sugar, salt, nor rice, and no clothing. They didn't even have rags to use when they menstruated. I drove two hundred miles to get sewing machines and Kotex for them.

Somehow this occasion, to come to Geneva to translate for such a powerful teacher, had seemed to me a reward for past service, assurance that I had worked off some of the harsh karma that had surrounded me.

Translating for Mr. Hodson had been such a pleasure that I couldn't believe how tired I was now. The last two nights of sleeplessness, nursing Mr. Schmidt, had taken their toll on me. The papers blurred before my eyes. I didn't know whether I was reading French or English. I felt I had reached the end of my endurance, yet I knew I must complete the work. I decided to stretch out on the little sofa and close my eyes for half an hour.

As I lay there, I glanced up at the window ledge and realized that the light coming through the window had brightened. In fact, rays of increasing brilliance were streaming in through the window. I could see the deep green branches of the large tree outside quite clearly, as if it were day.

I drew the library ladder underneath the window so that I could climb to the ledge to look out. My heart leaped. The light emanated from within the branches of the tree, and for two blocks the aura flooded the street. I felt it upon my face and upon my arms on the window ledge, and it filled me with a warm radiance. This unearthly light was familiar to me. I realized it came from a deva, a shining being.

Sometimes in dreams I had seen myself soaring in such a light on a mission to help someone in need. I had pulled a drowning woman from the sea; I had sent comfort to my sister in the hospital when she was frightened by a storm. Wingless, with a center so bright my eyes could not discern its shape, the deva shone from the tree. It poured through the library room like sunlight and spread a glow about the papers where I had been working, illuminating them. I realized that this was the light that is always around us, hidden from ordinary sight. The first meaning of the word *occult*, after all, is "hidden." The veil had been lifted for me.

I stepped down from the ladder, knelt on the carpet where I had spread the papers, and went back to work in that angelic radiance. I felt charged with energy. A gift of light takes you beyond time and its limitations. I believed it would enable me to work outside of time. And I was right. The shining being stayed with me the whole night long, and I was finished with my task by morning.

Kay Morris Seidell

Born April 4, 1904

Kay Morris, who was born in Petaluma, decided as a very young girl that she wanted to be a doctor; and in 1922, after finishing school, she entered the University of California Medical School. She served her residency at San Francisco General Hospital and in 1931 set up her general practice in Petaluma, where she is known all over town as Dr. Kay. She has been married almost fifty years to Stanley Seidell, a businessman, and they enjoy raising miniature roses and multitudes of vegetables. Another of her great pleasures is hiking with the Sierra Club.

Dr. Kay's practice began in the days when there were no antibiotics, and when the treatment for pneumonia included a mustard plaster on the chest, when she charged all of $3.50 for a house call. Since her retirement in 1969, she has maintained her license and frequently goes to medical seminars to remain current in her field. She participates in the American Cancer Society's Reach to Recovery program and gives consultations to women who have had breast surgery.

GROUP SUPPORT

Old age is ten years beyond your own chronological age.

—K.S.

The wry humor in the above statement is characteristic of Dr. Kay. For almost a decade she has been part of a remarkable support group of older women, who enjoy her humor *and* her sound sense. Her friend, Anna Keyes Neilsen (also in this volume) is another member of the group. The new Petaluma library provides space for the group, and the Reader's Forum is a Monday morning event shared by fifteen to twenty women.

The women are remarkable for their dissimilarities. Some earned their high school diplomas late in life at night school; a few, like Dr. Kay, are highly educated. They began to read and discuss everything from archaeology and Greek literature to stitchery, diary keeping, and vitamin therapy. (Dr. Kay's response to the vitamin enthusiast's faith in the value of vitamin therapy was in line with her training: a laconic "It's debatable.")

Dr. Kay was glad of the diary sessions, even though they were somewhat painful. She spoke laughingly of the process as a psychological evacuation, a high enema. The women started by writing autobiographies and reading them to one another; then they began to write diary entries on various subjects: memories; relationships with children, lovers, and teachers; their sexuality as they grow older—anything that vitally concerned them. "We were supposed to write in the diaries daily; most of us didn't do it every day," Dr. Kay confessed. But the results were considerable, nevertheless. "Our trust of each other developed, deepened. We became totally open with one another." Something happened in the group that was nourishing to all its members. "One woman was depressed," said Dr. Kay. "Her family had moved away. Obesity was a problem, and she'd considered suicide. Eventually she became totally revitalized." No longer just a few older women trying to keep mentally alert, the group became a dynamic, healing part of their lives.

Dr. Kay believes people everywhere ought to start something like their group. "Why waste a perfectly good life just sitting around wanting somebody to invite you to do something when you could get busy, do it yourself, and include some of your friends in it?"

The group decided to do a study of aging because they felt books they had read on the subject didn't fit what they knew. Daniel Levinson's *The Seasons of a Man's Life* was excellent but surveyed only men. Gail Sheehy's popular *Passages* seemed to presume that life ended in middle age and ignored the critical passage of retirement, except as something for which one must plan ahead. The ultimate passage of death was scarcely touched upon. The group wanted to know how people in their sixties and beyond felt about things, whether there were patterns of successful aging they could learn from. And so they circulated a questionnaire to about forty people over sixty. One member, Helen King, had a son who worked at the Smithsonian; he taught them how to do statistical samples.

Their findings balanced out on the plus side for the most part: leisure was a pleasure, and all of them enjoyed not having to compete. Few really saw themselves as old. That was when Dr. Kay made her wry comment: "Old age is ten years beyond your own chronological age." The older people were, the less they feared death, and there was an observable increase with each decade in faith in an afterlife.

Dr. Kay expressed some thoughts on that subject. "That is still an unfinished part

of me. I feel there's some role I have to play, and when that is finished, I'll be happy at the end of my life. I know that it has to do with religion. I think it's going to come to me. I was a Catholic the first thirty years of my life; after that, I wasn't. I couldn't stand the regimentation of convent schools. The real solution will be forthcoming."

Not only her childhood experience but her rationalist training inhibit the leap of faith at this point. "You get into such gobbledygook, that's what throws me. I think there is to me now such a thing as a soul, and how that's going to incorporate with the rest of things, I don't know, but that's my unfinished business."

Margaret Briggs Gardner

Born December 7, 1895

"There are friends waiting for you," her mother always said to Margaret Briggs and her four sisters when their father, an itinerant Methodist minister, had to move his family from one Indiana town to the next. It was good psychology, Margaret thinks, and undoubtedly her mother's reassurance gave her a personal security that is with her still. But the many moves of her childhood may have caused her to sink deep roots when she and her husband finally settled in the Berkeley hills. She attended both De Paul and Purdue universities, earning a bachelor's degree, after which she taught for a year, then worked as a chemist for a year. In 1922 she married Max W. Gardner, professor of plant pathology at Purdue. They had two children, a son, who is a horticulturist, and a daughter, a doctor of medicine.

In 1932 she and her husband moved into the house where she has lived ever since. He taught at the University of California at Berkeley and became chairman of the plant pathology department. After his death in 1979, Margaret continued to cultivate the garden they planted and cared for together, and which she describes as her great joy.

For many years she played the violin and enjoyed duets with her son, a pianist. She swims every other day with her long-time friend Alice Snyder (also in this volume).

GROWING THINGS

Her table was seated with old women. On the way into the garden club, two of the younger members had said to her, "Let's try to sit together." They liked her, she knew, had asked her advice about herbs at the last garden club meeting. One had been Max's student years ago, had married another botanist in the department. But once inside they were separated by an arrangement of placecards. Somebody had segregated the oldest members, herding them together at one table. Widows, every one of them. She had a seat next to Isabel, who couldn't garden any longer.

She would like to talk with people about gardening. Yesterday afternoon she got a good start for the spring. The bed hadn't been dug since the rains stopped. She was glad of her strength, that her hands were not impaired by arthritis. Her vision might keep her from her violin, but her hands could still pull weeds, turn a spade.

She had gone down the pathway lined with the stone wall her husband, Max, had put in years ago. Max had loved to make walls. She took a spade from the toolshed. The rose bushes, eaten in the fall by deer that came up through the little canyon below the house, were beginning to leaf out. She had tried planting things deer don't like—azaleas and daphne—but they got the rose leaves anyhow. This year she'd call a nursery to come in to spray the roses. She didn't trust her eyes with chemicals anymore—too easy to make a mistake. She didn't want to poison herself, but she wasn't going to give up on her roses. One of her young friends at the garden club would know the right place to call.

But here she was with the people who could no longer garden. It was pretty dull conversation, she thought, with people her own age. To get together and talk about what you can't see, can't hear, and where you can't go doesn't help a bit.

Isabel had not been feeling well for a long time. Her symptoms filled the mushroom soup, poured into the chicken salad, threatened dessert. When the club president rose and tapped a fork to her glass, Isabel didn't hear. Margaret nodded toward the platform, hoping Isabel would take notice. She knew her friend suffered. She knew, too, Isabel would probably decline more each passing year, that the multiplicity of her chronic ails went beyond the reach of cure. Margaret had a habit, if she felt a little low, of thinking of something she could do for someone else. Not much, just a simple gesture. Nothing that would call attention to itself. She did it for herself as much as for the other person. What could she do for Isabel? Suggest her own regimen—a morning swim, and in the afternoon an hour or so with the garden spade? Isabel never had exercised, even now that she was living in a retirement home where there were classes right downstairs. She would hoot at the notion that Margaret and Alice pick her up for a swim at the campus pool every day or so. In fact, Alice had offered not long ago to teach Isabel tap-dancing. "You could do it in a wheelchair," Alice had said. Poor Isabel, it probably would kill her.

Margaret thought of her last birthday, Alice's surprise party, planned beautifully in every detail. All her friends were there. Alice had made a Norwegian wreath cake in a hollow pyramid shape. There were snappers containing paper hats for everybody. That was like Alice, to have a regular kid's party. Thinking about it brought a sting to her eyes. My friends make my life, she thought.

The speaker, a woman in a pale print dress, had said something that made people laugh. Margaret leaned forward, hoping to catch a phrase or two, but all was drowned in the flood of Isabel's symptoms.

The speech was about horticultural therapy, so the card on the table said. That

gardening was being used on mental patients was something she'd like to know more about. She had always known it was good therapy. She turned up her hearing aid, but it only magnified Isabel's voice.

The speaker glanced briefly their way. Margaret placed her hand on Isabel's arm, pressed it gently. "I can't hear the speaker, dear."

Isabel said, "Neither can I. Not a word. I took my hearing aid back. If they don't work after the first two weeks, you don't have to pay for them."

She would go straight home, she decided, instead of to the bank as she should. She begrudged that trip to the bank to take care of the income-tax problem that had come up. She wasn't efficient with the bankbook, couldn't see the numbers without a magnifying glass. Max used to do all that. She didn't know why he hadn't trained her a bit more; the accounts had been all in his hands, and she had had complete confidence in him. They had just gone along, with no regard for the statistics that forecast that she would have it all to do one day. She would put off the bank business. Why go through another unpleasantness today? She had already missed learning about horticultural therapy.

At home she went straight to her garden. This was her delight, had been from the moment they bought the house just after Max began to teach at Berkeley years ago. Here they had planted their very lives.

She went past the ceanothus tree, blooming with its purple flowers. Max had planted it soon after they had bought the house. Most of the trees were his. She smiled, remembering how he used to bring wild trees from the woods so he could study their pathology. Specimens interested him, not landscaping. Instead of pulling weeds here, he was often out looking for diseases on weeds elsewhere. He'd bring home a little starving oak tree and plant it. There were tiny oaks all over for a while whose diseases he wanted to study. Some of them survived and still grew here in the garden, but he lost all interest in them once they were healthy. He was the scientist, and she, well, the laborer, she guessed.

She got into her work clothes right away and went outside. She took the spade and her garden gloves and went into the courtyard behind the house where impatiens abounded. She began to thin them out. The sound of Isabel's voice still rang in her ears, but she focused on her work. She loved plants. Like people, they depended on you; they were friends. If they became unhealthy, it was as if a friend were ill. She loved to see her garden flourish. Her own health depended on it.

She took the impatiens up to one of the beds near the outer wall Max had built and started turning the soil. Here there were oxalis. She pulled out some of them, but she was merciful to those with trumpet flowers, decided to let them stay. She would put chrysanthemum cuttings with them, and the impatiens. She would work this over and try to make it interesting. She loved to make a new bed.

She spaded and dug for—she didn't know how long. Was it an hour, or longer? She felt powerfully released from her frustration over not hearing the lecture. That's what her garden did for her.

She heard a sound in the kitchen. Inside she could glimpse the new student who had come to live in the house, a licensed deep-sea diver who was going into caves to photograph them. Spelunking. She was going to learn a lot from him.

How lucky she was! She had always been a happy woman. Perhaps Isabel hadn't been—could it be that simple? She didn't know if she herself could live in a retirement village with no garden as Isabel had to. But even there perhaps happiness would follow her.

She pulled off her gloves, flexing her strong wrists and fingers. Some lines from Byron came to her: "All who win joy must share it. Happiness was a born twin."

There was so much she could still enjoy. Tomorrow she would do some baking. She would bake a pie, perhaps take a piece of it to Isabel. A delicious fatigue spread through her body as she went inside to shower.

Klarna Pinska

Born January 7, 1902

Klarna Pinska's Russian parents failed to register the births of their children when they immigrated to Winnipeg, Canada, so in later years the five Pinska children did the best they could to reconstruct their birthdates. Klarna had to miss at least one engagement abroad as a dancer because of the problem with her birth certificate.

As far back as she can remember, Klarna wanted to be a dancer. When the great dancers came through Winnipeg, she went to watch them, trying to decide which one she wanted for her teacher. Ruth St. Denis was her choice from the moment she first saw her when she was eight. After her family immigrated to the United States and moved to San Francisco, Klarna went to Los Angeles and at fifteen auditioned for Miss Ruth, as the dancer's associates called her, and was accepted into her company. It became world renowned, both before and after her marriage to Ted Shawn, when the company became Denishawn.

After returning to San Francisco in the 1930s, Klarna began working in dance therapy. She taught the movement method developed by Bess Mensendieck to doctors and nurses at the University of California Medical Center. During World War II, she was a welder in the Sausalito shipyards and fought for the integration of the union (see Frances Mary Albrier in this volume).

Well known as a teacher, Klarna has taught at a number of universities, among them Duke, from 1981 to 1982, and Mills College, in 1983. When she was teaching at the University of California at Los Angeles in 1980, the National Endowment for the Arts funded a taped record of Klarna performing and teaching the St. Denis dances, which is still to be edited as a documentary.

KEEPER OF THE FLAME

Her sister said on the phone, "What! Are you still planning your career at eighty?"

Klarna sat at the table in her leotard, her tiny bare feet curled up on the rug. The table was a mountain of papers, forms, outlines, notes—it was enough to put you in the cuckoo house. In Miss Ruth's day there was no such thing as a grant proposal. You just struggled along, with maybe an occasional sponsor or patron. It was a different world now. The cost of a film about dance made it absolutely necessary for you to appeal to the foundations that offered their tantalizing grants—and their tiresome forms. "Brief Statement of Purpose." Boil down Miss Ruth to a hundred words or less? Ridiculous. It wasn't Klarna's nature to deal with these orderly demands.

Her nature was movement. She used to say, "I ran fast and never looked back."

And here were these forms making her look back. She told her sister it wasn't her own career, it was Miss Ruth's. The dances had already been taped at UCLA; funds had to be dug up from somewhere to edit the film, a record of the spirit of Denishawn.

But it *was* her career, her passion, her dedication. This is what her students were lacking. They just wanted to get up on a stage, didn't want to study for ten or fifteen years. That was one thing Klarna could do for them, remind them of what it really takes to be an artist—the devotion, the self-discipline.

"Aren't you a little young?" Miss Ruth had asked her when she was eight, in Winnipeg, and had made her appeal. More than anything in the world she wanted to be in Miss Ruth's dance company. At fifteen she made it. "You're not very pretty, child, so you'll have to work very hard." That was how Miss Ruth encouraged her. And bound her. Of course, she *was* pretty—delicate and light—but her size might be a drawback: she never grew over five feet nor weighed more than a hundred pounds. The invitation to work very hard was irresistible and became her way of life; whether onstage or off, she was Miss Ruth's handmaiden.

Miss Ruth was not a kind mentor; she was really very harsh when they were working. One student used to cry every day because she didn't understand Miss Ruth. It was so hard to keep up. One day it was Hinduism, the next the Tao, or the Rhythmic Choir, where they would light candles and play Eastern music; all that crystallized in the "Siddahs of the Upper Air," the last dance she and Ted Shawn created together. Along the way Miss Ruth made friends with Mary Baker Eddy and became a Christian Scientist.

There were times Klarna herself cried. After all, she was only fifteen at the start. Another girl in the company, mugging her face like a clown behind Miss Ruth's back, drew a snicker from Klarna, which in turn brought Miss Ruth's imperious command, "Leave the room, Klarna." You didn't defend yourself to Miss Ruth. Klarna burst into tears and fled from the studio, out of the building and into the streets, blindly running around the block.

The energy was there for her as soon as she returned, that powerful exchange of energy she always felt from Miss Ruth. She could lift you right out of yourself, turn you around, endow you with some of her own power. You paid her back, of course, with devotion. You did her bidding, ran out for her food, picked up her shawl, wrote her letters, whatever she asked.

And when there was no work, you tore yourself away from her, took jobs dancing wherever you could, in the Rockland Terrace Cafe in Brooklyn, where Al Capone hung out with his henchmen and gave silver-dollar tips. Or at a dive on Fifty-first Street, where a famous female impersonator asked, "My dear, what is a nice Jewish girl like you doing in this place?" Such a far cry from the intensity, the aesthetic purity of Miss Ruth's choreographies.

In later years Klarna once asked Miss Ruth if she ever thought of her as a woman. Miss Ruth said, "What do you mean, child?" Klarna said, "You never talked to me as a woman." Her reply: "You're one of the people in the world, one of the women, who become more beautiful as you grow older." She could come out with things like that.

She often spoke of creating a new center of the dance where that energy would work for other young dancers, but it never came about. She wanted to found a Church of the Divine Dance and to organize a dancing choir with women over fifty. She had so many plans. Some people said she wasn't interested in the careers of other dancers, didn't really want to encourage them. But if you had ever worked with her as Klarna had, you knew the magical energy was there for all her company. It was true that you had to save yourself at some point; you had to leave your teacher, create your own life.

Eventually her protegées scattered. Klarna had been teaching dance therapy in San Francisco when she heard of Miss Ruth's accident. She had gone with Pearl Wheeler to Yosemite, where their automobile crashed. Over ninety and still a Christian Scientist, Miss Ruth refused medical treatment for her injured knee. When she danced thereafter, she could move only one leg. Yet she went on. Dancing with only one knee, Miss Ruth was still a triumph. "Dance begins in consciousness, not in the body," she said.

She asked Klarna to come and stay with her in a little house her brother had provided for her; she was lonely, afraid she would be forgotten. But Klarna knew her own limitations; she could visit her every month, but she could not live with her. In her old age Miss Ruth needed even more attendance. She got hold of you, wrenched your life away from you. She couldn't help it; she always needed a handmaiden. Even in the hospital, where a heart attack finally took her away, she had ordered the doctors about like flunkies, sending one of them to fetch her makeup.

Too upset to go to the funeral, Klarna grieved alone. It was 1968. Memories poured back. She had come to Miss Ruth as a child, and now she was in her midsixties. She had devoted her life to working with the principles she had learned from her teacher. Everywhere she taught, every performance she gave she moved under the inspiration of Ruth St. Denis. Now it was over. The dance was an ephemeral art, movement in time and space, then over so quickly. Like a moment in life of remembered perfection.

Years before, in Boston, Klarna had danced "Sonata Pathétique," the piece some people thought was a women's liberation dance, which was choreographed for Doris Humphrey. It was Doris's own dance, and when Klarna looked down into the audience, there were Doris and Charles Weidman. Throughout the entire piece tears had streamed from Klarna's eyes. These were precious, ephemeral moments in her own life. Miss Ruth in the wings, telling another woman in the company, "That is the way 'Sonata Pathétique' is supposed to be danced." Afterward Doris and Charles saying they never saw such a "Sonata Pathétique." "*There* is a dancer," they said.

Klarna left her table, needing her morning exercise more than usual with all this paperwork. She had to stretch and bend, move. But she would go on with this wretched task of seeking a grant. The dances must be preserved, and Klarna had the commitment she missed in the young. She was the keeper of the flame.

Cecil Pierce

Born October 22, 1908

When Cecil Pierce retired from her job as seamstress for Highland Hospital, where she made surgical gowns and mended sheets, she had no idea that she would become an actress. Yet acting with the College Avenue Players has taken her all over the West Coast. Produced by Stewart Kandell and directed by Linda Spector, the Players were designed for seniors, audience and performers, although they now play for schoolchildren as well as for Shakespeare festivals. Frankly polemical, the company's intention is to fight agism in all forms; it is intergenerational and interracial. Cecil said that when Kandell recruited her, he named three misconceptions about elders—that they don't have fun, that they lack energy, that they can't memorize. Cecil takes lecithin and never forgets a line. The company does more than a hundred performances a year.

Cecil was born in New York City. She married in 1931 and some years later moved with her husband to California. The had a daughter who was handi-capped, and in order to stay at home with her child, Cecil started a dress-making business. When her child was older, she worked as a home health aide, and after that as a seamstress. Although they divorced in 1961, she and her husband are good friends and often go to the theater together.

Besides acting, Cecil explores other creative activities; she plays the organ, sketches, and paints.

In the seventeenth century Margaret Cavendish, Duchess of Newcastle, wrote of the artistry in "woman's work." Giving a new shape to things is finding the foundation of art, but for women such activity had to be useful. Needlework such as quilting and embroidery, china painting, and even making straw flowers served a function in the home, more firmly defining woman's place. In recent years museum shows have paid tribute to these arts, as historians explore their value in the culture. In Cecil Pierce we see how the suppressed artist, always diverted by tasks of necessity, works to emerge in the freedom of her late years.

LAUGHTER

The children shriek with delight. They love the sassy tongue of Cecil's Cinderella as she talks back to her stepsisters. Cinderella must have had some spunk—she got the prince, didn't she?

The kids also enjoy the fact that the show's Cinderella is over seventy. And black. Cecil further enjoys messing up people's expectations by wearing a blonde wig that complements her amber skin and eyes.

Before the play Cecil has shown them her sketches of street people, which she keeps in an album with plastic jackets, more than a hundred sketches. The children laugh in recognition. They, too, ride the buses. Cecil has captured a broad rear end as it exits from a bus, and other outrageous folks, such as a pudgy woman wearing an Oreo cookie pendant, and a bulky bag-lady with a Safeway cart.

A week ago they played for this same group of sixth graders, a skit entitled "Was There Life Before TV?"—a dialogue between children and grandparents about entertainment of other eras. Before today's performance the teacher tells the actors that the students have something to show them later.

Cecil never dreamed of being an actress. But two years ago a woman who later became her friend struck up a conversation with her at a bus-stop bench. Cecil had gone to Guy's Drugs for a special on MJB Rice and happened to have her sketchbook with her. Usually Cecil drew from memory. Across the street a man stood in bare feet, with huge suspendered trousers hauled up over his belly; he was shirtless, with a loose tie at the neck. She opened her sketchbook and quickly outlined his shape. The woman sitting next to her asked to see it.

Somehow the woman, Ann, persuaded Cecil to go with her to an art class at a senior center. Cecil had never seen herself as the type to go to a senior center, but since her retirement, she had noticed a tendency in herself to experiment. And now, thinking in "types" was an act of the enemy. Stewart had come into art class one day and asked for volunteers for his acting company. Cecil thought, I've always had a bit of the ham in me, and agreed to give it a try.

Now she had traveled all up and down the West Coast, had even acted in a training film with some of the other players. How much stronger they had all become with this activity. Cecil had noticed it in the other actors as well as in herself—higher energy.

After the performance, the children bring out their surprise. They have made a collection of things belonging to their grandparents. One child has brought a quilt with a tree-of-life design that her grandmother made. Another has a stereopticon that had been her grandfather's. Another, a phonograph; cranked up, it plays Caruso.

Maybe the play has helped the kids learn something about life before TV, Cecil thinks. At least this means they've been talking to their grandparents.

One of the kids opened her book of sketches again and called a friend to see: a young man drinking rum in a Safeway line. On the next page a blond woman in a T-shirt that reads: "Hot Day in January." And then a woman playing a piano: her belly is so large it spills onto the keys. Hindu, Asian, black, or white—no group is spared by Cecil's merciless crayons. The children laugh.

"Why are so many of them so fat?" a little girl wonders.

Cecil laughs. "I *know* them, that's why. I used to fit dresses on such people when I was a seamstress."

Outsize clothing used to be her specialty. Large women from all over the Bay Area had come to her. She had taken supersize measurements a thousand times. "And I put the women in clothes that suited them, smocks and tailored dresses, not those tight knits and harlequin pants nobody has any business wearing."

One of the girls asks her, "Do you still sew?"

"Well, I made my costume."

"Did you make the other costumes too?" Her friends in the cast laugh at that.

Cecil says, "Not a chance. I am not getting stuck behind a sewing machine ever again."

Ada Cutting Perry

Born October 27, 1880   Died September 27, 1983

I feel I still have one more adaptation to make, to death.
—A.C.P. at 100

Ada Perry lived to be almost one hundred and three. She was born in New York State, near Watertown, and started to train as a nurse in her early twenties but stopped in order to work as a nurse-companion for a well-to-do family. A young relative they invited to a party on their houseboat on the Hudson River fell in love with Ada and asked her to marry him.

After their marriage in 1905, his family fortunes went into reverse, and Ada and her husband moved to a ranch in the White Mountains in Owens Valley, California, near Mono Lake. There her husband raised alfalfa and worked in the neighborhood as a carpenter. They had five children; her youngest daughter, Barbara, was born when she was forty-seven, so Ada was raising a very young child during her menopause.

Life on the ranch was rigorous; the narrow gauge railroad came through and dropped household supplies when the Perrys could afford them, but most food was homegrown. Ada's children remember that she cooked batches of baked beans and bread to sell to neighbors. She was constantly preparing meals for cattlemen and alfalfa hands. And she also found time to help nearby Indian women to read and to write letters to their children who had been sent away to Indian school. She taught her own children to read and write too, and when they were older and went away to school in Riverside, she sent laundered shirts to her sons each week through the mail.

In 1944, when her husband became ill, they moved north to Berkeley to live with their oldest son, George, a bachelor. In her sixties then, with a teenage daughter, Ada developed her strong gifts of adaptation. It was a theme she thought about a lot in her later years, how each decade brought a new adaptation for her to make.

ONE HUNDRED GIFTS

I realize I am always adapting to the next lesson in life. I have been old now for more than thirty years. I thought I was old at seventy, but then thirty more years have just flown away. I've had a lot of adapting to do with each decade.

The ranch was a big adaptation for me when I was a young wife. I never made a glowing success at that, no matter what my children say. The life was so different for me. There were a lot of crop failures, floods. One year the water system gave out entirely during a flood, and we were without water for two weeks, hauled it from our neighbors' place. And then you never knew how many people might be there for dinner, or who they were. It was very difficult training for me. Very instructive. But the scenery was beautiful, the Sierra Nevada on one side, the White Mountains on the other. I did my best to adapt.

I had always been interested in birds when we lived in Owens Valley. There was such a variety of western birds about the ranch, but there wasn't time then to learn much about them. Well, after we had moved here to Berkeley, my husband died; and while I was overcoming my grief, I began to watch the birds outside my window and in the garden quite closely. I learned such a lot about them; it was another world.

Then after seventy, I couldn't see the birds very well, so I turned to plants. Taking care of indoor plants, close work like that I could still do.

And haiku—I even took a turn at writing poetry once my eyes weakened and I couldn't read as well as before. A friend and I had a go at that. My daughter-in-law had some greeting cards made of one of my haiku poems. She did the calligraphy. They were so pretty that I've never even used them.

I've kept changing my activities to fit my physical limitations. In my eighties I adapted to not going out so much as before.

One thing that's nice to do around the house is canning. George and I pick the raspberries in the backyard and put them up. My daughter-in-law came in the other day and found me on the stepladder taking down the large kettle we boil them in and tried to make me stop. But I always remember it's important to have some work to do. George understands that. He's the only one of my children who has never married. It touches me to see him growing older, my bachelor son, to realize that he has almost caught up with me, is as old now as I was when I realized I was an old woman.

On my one hundredth birthday I got three letters of congratulations in the mail: one from my congressional representative, one from the governor of the state, and one from the Oval Office. They must have my number. I also received a package from a woman who published a history of the church in which my father was a minister. When I opened it, I found that inside it were a hundred gifts. Cologne, a paper of pins, a box of dusting powder, bubble bath, gloves, stockings, toys. For weeks, every time one of the grandchildren came, we'd open another batch of presents.

I don't feel too different about being a hundred. After all, it's just a matter of good health and circumstance. I'm glad that I still have the use of my legs, my arms, my hands, my brain. I'm so thankful for common everyday health. I'm hungry, I enjoy food, and I love to eat something that's not good for me.

I have one more adaptation I must make in life, then I'll be through. It's something I don't talk to a lot of people about because most of them would be bored with it. But

I want to adapt to the idea of death. It's important that I shouldn't be afraid of death. There's not as much fear as there was twenty years ago, but I still have work to do. There's a certain laziness that I'm anxious to overcome. I should just go about it calmly and get on better terms with death. I hope I can adapt to it as well as I have to everything else. It might be around the corner.

I still get angry, and that's part of the fear, I think. I have these strong angers over nothing. I just flare up. I hope my children don't remember me for my anger when I'm gone.

I have a book, *The Book of Ancient Prayers*, that is helping me. All through the ages people have gone through the fear of death, and there has always been a belief that God would be with us when we die. It has been a teaching throughout the world in all religions —that we don't have to be afraid of death, that we can accept it as we accept birth.

My religion has helped me, even if I still have a ways to go. The only one of my children who doesn't share my faith is George. We have teased about it now and then, but I leave him alone now. It's an individual matter. There's nothing of the missionary about me. I always hoped I wouldn't narrow into rigid thinking and force my religion on my family, which I think is being a bore and assuming too much. I prefer to be an example in the way I live, if I can.

My religion has brought me happiness and relief, and I've never had that desperate despair so many people seem to struggle with as they grow old. I am so thankful for ordinary things.

Pure water lily
how grew you
so white
Rising through
dark water?
—Ada C. Perry

Eleanor Milder Lawrence

Born November 23, 1910

Eleanor Milder was born and raised in San Francisco. She began photographing when she was seventeen. She saved money for years to go to college but spent it instead on her first Graflex camera. Finally she did go to college, then returned when she was in her sixties for a bachelor's degree from University of California in the school of environmental design. Attending at the same time was her daughter, Susan, whom she adopted during her second marriage. She has one grandchild. Her sister was the popular folk singer Malvina Reynolds.

In 1952 she married her present husband, Thompson Lawrence. For many years she has been well known for her nature photography. She collected some of her work in the volume By the Way, *published in 1980. During 1983-84, she was president of San Francisco Women Artists.*

In 1970 Eleanor was hospitalized by a stroke. The spirit of her work as a photographer is reflected in the story of her recovery.

RETURN

Eleanor could see that the small dark nurse standing behind the doctor reacted strongly to what he had said, was clearly shocked by his words, their finality. He had looked straight down at her and said, "There can be no hope of recovery from this."

Words were exploding behind her own eyes, pressing against the roof of her mouth and jamming at the barrier of her teeth. None escaped into sound. This was the source of the doctor's assurance, her own incapacity. He stood blandly over her, announcing her doom as if he were a television weatherman—tomorrow cloudy, no change in sight. She could *see* everything; her eyes were gulping down the world. It was incredible that she could give none of it back again—impossible.

Delivered of his diagnosis, the doctor departed. Just like that. A cold wind stirring through the door.

The nurse stayed behind, went to the door, looked outside, then closed the door behind her. A little woman, Filipina perhaps, with a fierce face. Eleanor, at sea in her thoughts, paid no attention to her at first.

In that sea she struggled among images from her life. She had been afloat for nearly seventy years, swimming with long, even strokes, especially in her later years.

How frightened Tom had been when he brought her here to Kaiser. They had just come back from a trip to Samarkand, hadn't even had time to call Susan. Now he would be phoning her in Pasadena, and she would be rushing here, frightened. Tom was to go back to work the day it happened. The doctor had said he'd call him if there was any change. She could see Tom now at the garden center, where people took their gardening problems to him: "Yes, the creature on this leaf is an aphid." "For leaf curl you need to spray the tree in latency." He never had time for a garden of his own.

She couldn't believe what the doctor had said. Would she be helpless for years to come? She thought of how she used to drive to Marin on picture-taking trips. Would she never take another picture, yet go on drawing in the images that had always pulled her to her camera—the way an ivy hangs from a wall, encircles a door like a wreath; the way the tules float above a sky-filled lake; the way a plum on its stem readies itself to fall; or the way leaves force themselves to bud from a rotten branch? Or was it worse? It wasn't any easier for her to imagine the world without herself in it than it was for the blade of grass she had photographed as it forced its way through a crack in the sidewalk.

"It isn't so!" The voice of the little nurse reached her. She was leaning over the bed, her face very angry. "He shouldn't have said that!" The nurse was whispering furiously. Recovery *was* possible. She had seen it *often* in people who put their will into it. "I couldn't believe he was saying that!" she cried.

The sea in her mind quieted under the nurse's gaze. A tremendous sense of confidence welled up in her. Of course, she *knew* the nurse was right. Relief flooded her, and she became possessed of a single thought: recovery. The nurse stayed with her for an hour, talked with her, encouraged her. She learned of a rehabilitation center in Vallejo where stroke victims were given intensive treatment. The doctor could send her there.

One of her photographs came back: a goose caught after poking its head between fence slats, stuck, unable to see a way out. Silly goose, it only needed a little guidance from someone with a larger picture, then its neck would be free.

She loved to make photographs because there are certain beautiful things in the world that need to be recorded before they go away. Everything is ephemeral; nothing is the same from one moment to the next, whether because of light or time or weather. She was no different. She didn't have to stay frozen in this sea of memory—that was her doctor's idea, one she would not adopt.

That night she slept soundly, dreamlessly. The next morning she glanced down at her hand on the white sheet. Two fingers on her right hand flickered. Watching her hand, she willed it to happen again. Slowly her forefinger lifted, then her second finger.

Susan arrived in the afternoon, came into the room cautiously, her husband with her. He was in medical school down south, and she so wanted to tell them they needn't stay. She would be all right. Tom was with them, and all were veiling their fear with a surface of concern.

No doubt Tom had spoken with the doctor, heard his unilateral decision. If only she could tell them, reassure them. If only they could see how unafraid she felt now, how confident.

They stayed all day, but nothing moved. Their faces grew drawn with fatigue and fear. She wanted to tell them to go home to rest, that everything would be all right. A ghost might feel like this, longing to reassure a loved one.

But there was no way to tell them. This was her own struggle, hers alone. A trial perhaps, but she felt, *knew*, she was not finished yet.

It happened slowly, bit by bit, always when she was alone, like a confirmation that it was her own task. Her sister would come, many of her friends, and yet she lay immobile. In her moments alone the little movements occurred.

On the third day her speech returned. She was so relieved that she forgave her doctor. She told him haltingly, half in fun, "You'd better get me to the rehabilitation center or I won't need it."

By the tenth day she was able to lift her right hand up to her chest. Her bed was cranked up so that she was nearly in a sitting position. She could look down at her hand and see it there, as if it were waiting. She knew what it was waiting for.

The next day she lifted the right hand to her chest again, this time much more easily. And then her left hand moved; she raised it slowly, inch by inch, until at last it was very nearly parallel with her right. Two more inches and she'd have it—there! Both hands, a few inches separating them just below her heart.

She would make it now, she knew. A deep sigh went through her. It would be all right, just a matter of time and effort. She wanted to tell her family, the nurse, everyone, just what it meant to her to lift her hands in that gesture with just enough space to hold her camera. That was how she knew she wasn't finished. She could go back to work again.

Anna Keyes Neilsen

Born February 26, 1903

The enthusiasm of a beautiful woman can be a great spur to a man's work, and for most of her life, Anna Neilsen provided that support for her husband. Just after college, at the University of California at Berkeley, she married a small-town doctor in Petaluma and for many years was his office assistant. They had two daughters, and Anna has four grandchildren. When her husband's health forced his retirement, she nursed him for five years before his death.

Since becoming a widow in her early seventies, Anna has discovered in herself an extraordinary range of interests. Her lifelong friend Kay Seidell said, "There're lots of things to do, Anna," and she told her where to buy a good piece of luggage with wheels. Anna has traveled with it thousands of miles. She continues to take part in many of the volunteer activities identified in her generation with the wives of professionals —providing food and distributing clothing for those in need and visiting some of her husband's former patients, who are now in nursing homes. She also does typing and sewing for the local Cinnabar Theater. However, she says that *she arranges her life now so that no one will become too dependent upon her— the soup kitchen won't go under if she isn't there. She is free for the many journeys she wants to make.*

Although she travels a great deal, many of her journeys are of the mind. She meets regularly with fifteen to twenty older women (see Kay Morris Seidell in this volume for a more complete description of the group) who study a broad range of subjects, including archaeology, painting, and philosophy. She and her older sister, Bess, live in different towns, but they occasionally meet to enjoy an Elderhostel, the summer educational program for people over sixty that has more than 80,000 participants throughout the world. Recently she has studied women's self-defence and done gliding and ballooning; the latter, she says, is the less exciting of the two.

The story she told about river rafting with her grandson says a lot about the caring family's delicate balance; responsibility toward elders may interfere with their freedom. Anna's blend of affection, candor, and assertiveness helps her maintain the independence she needs.

PRECIOUS DAYS

When Anna came in from the theater, the flyer from Oars had arrived in the mail, and she called outside to Jason to tell him about it. This summer she wanted to take him on another rafting trip, just the two of them. He would be fifteen, and she eighty-two. Maybe this would be the last year he'd want to do a thing like that with his grandmother.

He grinned at her from the backyard. His teeth were looking beautiful now that his braces were off, and he'd grown another four inches since she'd seen him last. She was happy that her house, with all the trees in the back, was pleasant for him to visit. He seemed to love getting away from New York for his winter vacation.

"How about the Middle Fork of the American this year, Jason?" she asked. "Around mid-August looks like a good trip."

She'd be back then from the Elderhostel she and her sister were planning. That would be good for Bess, who was doing a lot of drawing these days. One of the courses was Sketching Your Journey. She herself felt like an inept kindergartner in such a class, but the other course, on modern poetry, was appealing. She enjoyed the people who went to the Elderhostels; they were from all kinds of backgrounds, strong individuals who were still open to new ideas. The one she went to last year at the Shakespeare festival had renewed her passion for the theater, and she'd plunged into local work backstage.

Jason handed back the rafting schedule. "Sounds okay." He was far from enthusiastic. Maybe the time when he felt like going somewhere with Nana had already come and gone. Maybe he had learned that her feet were made of clay. She had to be sensitive to that. Even as a child, Anna had felt determined she would never become a crabby, disagreeable old person, as the elders around her had been. She didn't have a lot of time with her family; it was pretty farflung for frequent visits, with Jason and Shirley in New York and Gloria in Los Angeles. But they had always enjoyed being together. So far she hadn't experienced any "old lady aversion." Jason had never shown the least reluctance to be around her until now—if that is what his attitude meant.

"What's wrong, Jason? Rafting lost its appeal?"

"No, no. It'll be swell." Then he asked if she weren't going to be busy working for the little theater this summer. Jason knew better. She wouldn't even take roles with the company because she didn't want to make extended commitments of her time now that it was all hers and not her husband's or her family's. She limited herself to being theater flunky. She'd told Jason her attitude before. Something was definitely wrong.

They had become white-water rafting enthusiasts eight years ago, when Shirley called to invite her to join her and Jason in Utah for a trip down the Colorado. She immediately said yes. When Shirley told it later to her friends, she put in a pause in which the listener was supposed to imagine Anna's thinking: At my age? Seventy-four at the time. But everybody adds a touch of fiction to a story. The truth was, Anna didn't hesitate a moment.

From Utah they flew by small plane down into the Grand Canyon, and for three days and nights they were taken completely out of their own lives. At night they lay looking up at the colored tiers of the earth's history, united to the universe of stars and filled with a sense of peace and mystery. By day the excitement, especially on the rapids, took all bounds out of existence. She loved the movement of the earth speeding past them, the sensation of the water drenching her face and hair. Later when friends asked, "Weren't you afraid of the white water?" She answered, "Yes, that's why you go. For those moments that is all there is to life, just hanging on and feeling it."

On that first trip the raft was enormous; it held all thirty-two people in the party, and there were moments when it seemed to lift straight up into the air. Jason was still small enough to cling to her and to his mother, shrieking with delight. The pleasure children take in being afraid—rafting restored that forgotten joy to her life.

Last summer, when they went together to ride the North Fork of the American River, just the two of them, the rapids weren't nearly as high. The party was broken up into four rubber rafts, which young women were paddling quite competently. Yet there was plenty of white water; they were all wet to the skin most of the time, their tennis shoes soaked. Jason often sat straddling the ballooning side of the rubber raft, and whenever it got rough, he slid down beside her, held onto her. It wasn't as rigorous a trip as the Colorado, they had agreed, but still those were a few precious days she wouldn't forget.

Maybe Jason felt differently, thought it hadn't been exciting enough? At night they had slept outdoors in their sleeping bags. On the second morning Jason expressed the worry that had kept both of them from drifting immediately to sleep: "What if a bear had come?" —almost as if he wanted a scare. Maybe the water was just too tame after the Colorado.

She put it to him. They had no secrets from one another. If he wanted to go on some other river, she wanted to know. And if he felt he was too old to go with her, she wanted to know that too.

"Oh, Nana, it's just that—well, Aunt Gloria was just as bad as Mom about things last year." Gloria—what did she have to do with it? Jason was looking down at his large feet.

Finally she dug it out of him. Both his mother and his aunt had made him promise to look after her whenever the water got rough. She remembered that he'd always come to grasp her hand during the rapids, but she hadn't imagined it was on his mother's and aunt's instructions. Those two girls! "Jason, that's ridiculous. It must have spoiled the trip for you."

"I didn't want to tell you because they were just worried about you, that's all."

It wasn't fair to put that kind of pressure on a child when he was supposed to be enjoying himself. And she knew Jason, a child who took his responsibilities seriously.

"Don't say anything to them about it," Jason pleaded. He could see how annoyed she was. And now he was taking more responsibility, asking her not to reproach them. What was the answer? She had to make sure she had the whole story, that the boy would otherwise enjoy the trip with her.

She had worried about old age since she was a child, never having seen anybody aging gracefully. At twenty-one she had decided that chess would keep her mind alert and had learned the game for her old age. She had also studied braille, though she didn't know if she would remember it now. She was determined never to dampen the spirits of anybody younger than she. Maybe she spread herself thin, but it was better than becoming a bore.

What Jason said next told her what she needed to know. "Nana, I'll just come out here and stay with you a while, how about that? We can play chess. I'm getting better at it."

"Jason, let's make a pact," she said. "I want to go rafting. I think you do too. Let's tell Oars we want them to put us on separate rafts. We can trade notes at night, and bunk together to protect each other from bears. How does that sound?"

"Gosh, Nana, I don't know . . ."

"Just one condition. We won't tell your mother or Aunt Gloria about our pact."

He hesitated a moment, then his grin sealed their conspiracy.

Haruko Obata

Born February 10, 1892

When she was ten years old, Haruko came to San Francisco, and soon afterward she began her lifelong study of ikebana, flower arranging. Other crafts interested her as well, and in high school she learned to make dress patterns, which did not exist in Japan. On a visit to her family in Tokyo, she went on a lecture circuit to introduce American fashion patterns there. The tour was a great success and did much to bring Western clothing design to Japan. In 1912 she married Chiura Obata, a professor of art at the University of California at Berkeley, who became a world-renowned sumi-e painter. There is an Obata family story about a Chiura Obata exhibit in which a silk scroll, Mother Earth, was first hung. Eighty-six inches high, it is a nude, a pregnant woman in profile, with long black hair down her back, the full golden contour of her belly. Haruko was embarrassed by it, fearful of being recognized as the model. She was only twenty. But at the opening she removed all doubt herself by telling everyone who came just who the model was.

Haruko was teaching flower arranging to WAC officers at the time her family was taken for internment, first to Tanforan, then to Topaz, Utah. Her daughter and older son went with them, but her younger son adamantly refused to go to the camps. After much effort on the part of his parents, he was admitted instead to St. Louis University, where he graduated at the end of the war. He is Gyo Obata, a distinguished architect, who designed the National Air and Space Museum in Washington, D.C., the Dallas–Fort Worth Airport, the Moscone Convention Center in San Francisco, and many other internationally known buildings. Before the war's end, a professor at St. Louis University sponsored the release of the Obata family, and they remained in St. Louis until the war ended. There Haruko worked as a window dresser and made many ikebana designs.

After the war, her husband resumed his teaching at the university. She continued to teach ikebana; in fact, she still goes to the Enshu School in Japan for occasional study. She and her husband sponsored Obata Tours for many years, traveling with Americans to visit the art treasures of Japan. In 1975 the emperor of Japan honored her with an award for her outstanding contribution to her community in this country.

In recent years Haruko and her granddaughter Kimi Kodani, an advertising artist, have been sharing the house in Berkeley where Haruko's classes in ikebana are held.

THE WAY OF THE FLOWER

The yellow greasewood vase her mother made in the internment camp stood on the table. Yuri remembered seeing her make it from a piece of salvaged firewood, polishing the gnarled and twisted trunk, carving a hollow out of its center for flowers. Today she would use it in the flower show. Magnolia buds that looked like giant pussy willow and quince flowers were spread beside the vase.

Her mother had a new student, an older Caucasian woman, who was doing it all wrong. The new student was jamming her vase too full, so her mother was starting at the beginning, explaining the principles of ikebana. She said, "These three—heaven, man, and earth—three different planes but united in one form." A few deft strokes with her hands and clippers and the design was reduced to more graceful proportions.

Yuri had dropped by to make sure her mother had a ride to the show. Her daughter Kimi was away for the weekend. She was glad it suited Kimi to live here. They made a good team, grandmother and granddaughter, gave each other space and support and only occasional direction, such as when Kimi would find her grandmother's friends in Japanese conversation she knew concerned her own marital status. She was already in her late twenties and unmarried!

Her mother told the new student to put the rest of the magnolia buds into her car. "I will ride with you. We can talk." Apologetically the woman said her car was a mess. "Don't worry about that. I'm ninety-two and have ridden in everything, even a hearse."

Topaz, Utah, the internment camp. Yuri was only thirteen and had seen her mother ride away in the hearse to gather shrubs and wildflowers for the classes she taught in the camp. The funny mayor of the little nearby town was also the local undertaker. When she had no flowers, she taught her students to make them of paper. Sometimes flowers came all the way from a florist in Hayward, California.

Her parents believed that wherever they were they had to stimulate art, so as soon as they were taken to Tanforan, even in their initial internment, they had started teaching art and ikebana. She would never forget how the entire family was quartered at Tanforan racetrack, in a single horse stall. The odor of the hay stuck in the cracks of the stall would remain forever in her memory. When it rained, water leaked in so that they were up to their knees in mud.

It had grieved her parents that many of the older people were so stunned by the camps, so despondent. They wanted to offer them the uplift and consolation of art. She knew how strong her parents were because when they were sent to the camp in Utah— where families were undermined by the mess halls; where families were not even allowed to eat together; where there were gangs of vehement, reckless teenagers—their family remained united.

Her parents gave themselves not only to art but to reason as well, as when the camp meetings began, and the disputes between the Yes-Yes groups and the No-No's tore at the heart of the people. In those meetings the No-No's, many Japanese-born, were adamantly opposed to signing the loyalty oath of their captors. Yet her father spoke out against them, tried to reassure the people that compliance was the obligation of a citizen.

One evening when he went out of the barracks to the shower stalls, he was struck on the forehead and thrown down on the gravel walk. His assailant might have killed him, except that her father grasped a handful of gravel and flung it up in the darkness. It must have struck the man's face, for he dropped the lead pipe with which he had attacked and turned and ran. She remembered how her father had come into their room with his padded robe pressed over his eye. He told her mother, "Lock yourselves inside—I am going to the hospital," and he left.

The pipe had struck his eye socket, and the eye didn't heal properly. Finally the camp authorities agreed to let him go to the hospital in Salt Lake City and to let Yuri and her mother leave the camp as well. She would never forget the bathrobe her mother showed her, its padding covered with blood. The new student asked her mother what she meant about riding in a hearse. Mother explained about the mayor-undertaker. "He used to joke about the hearse and say I ought to hire him as my permanent chauffeur. 'Look at all the room we have for flowers in the back,' he'd say." She lifted the yellow greasewood vase. "You'll see others like this at the show," she said. She told everyone to take their ikebana to their cars. Yuri told her mother she would stay to clear away the cuttings.

The new student's next move was to lift her arrangement from the cut-glass vase and wrap it in the newspaper spread out on the table for trimmings. Then in embarrassment she realized how carefully everyone else was taking their arrangements with them. The woman shook her head. "I may be too old to learn flower arranging," she said.

"Oh no," was the humorous reply. "Ikebana is older than you, *very* old. Buddha was supposed to have had ikebana on his throne. If you know flower arranging, you do not grow old, for it is eternal."

Joan Bridge Baez

Born April 11, 1913

Joan Bridge Baez is always responsive to appeals for help, and they have taken her as far as Cambodia and Somaliland.

"I'm not a starter of things," Joan says, "but I don't have to be because I have so many powerful people in my life who are." She mentioned a few: her former husband, the physicist Albert Baez, who worked with UNESCO for many years; the late Rosemary Goodenough, who persuaded Soledad prison to let inmates build a playground for their children's visits, a playground where Joan volunteered to work with the kids; Kay Boyle, the writer, who led protests against the draft and U.S. support of the Shah of Iran; her daughter Mimi Farina, a well-known singer who founded Bread and Roses, an organization devoted to entertaining shut-ins; and her daughter Joan Baez, whose widespread activities for the causes of peace and human rights and her folksinging career have kept her too busy to answer fan mail, a task she herself has always cheerfully undertaken. She makes regular visits to nursing homes. "If I want to feel young, I can always do something for someone older than myself," she said wryly.

Born in Edinburgh, Scotland, Joan Bridge immigrated to Canada with her family as a child, where her mother died. Her father, an itinerant Episcopal minister, took Joan and her sister throughout the United States; he later became a professor of English and drama at Hunter College, then at Grinnell. That early life of travel foreshadowed her marriage; Albert Baez's teaching and consulting work took them all over the world, to Baghdad, Iraq, England, and Paris. He was on the faculty at Stanford University; so their three daughters—Pauline, Mimi, and Joan—were raised mostly in California. Divorced late in life, she said, "I just don't want to live with anybody." Her former husband still enjoys her friendship, and her new freedom has given her time for writing the family memoir she has had in mind for some time.

Actually she is moved by a powerful social consciousness of her own, which took her to Thailand in 1979, where the International Rescue Committee built a camp to help the thousands of Cambodian refugees whose government was engaged in a mass slaughter of civilians suspected of dissent. Her daughter Joan's organization, Humanitas International, which devotes itself to giving direct aid in distressed international situations, had sent some trucks and buses to the camp, which were used, among other things, to transport volunteers from town to their work at the camp.

CHILDREN OF WAR

Soon after the truck set Joan down in the refugee camp, a young Thai girl appeared wanting to talk about "Choanie." Her name was Nini. She had been to the Joan Baez concert there in Thailand, was a fan. She came to the back of the large hospital tent, which was made of bamboo stalks covered with blue plastic, where Joan and her partner, Rosemary Taylor, were sewing by hand. Nini sat down on a bed opposite them beside a pile of print fabrics. She chattered about Choanie, dazzled. Surely Choanie's mother must share some of the luster of her famous daughter.

Rosemary, an Australian volunteer, had welcomed Joan when she arrived a few days earlier. ("Oh, am I getting some help? How nice. Cup of coffee?") She was a dark-haired Australian woman, her hair in two braids. Relieved by her friendly, good-natured manner, Joan had immediately started to work with her. Rosemary had helped her recover from the shock of entering the camp.

Khao I Dang, "Beautiful Mountain." It rose in the distance, above a thick cloud of dust. More like a backdrop for hell, Joan had thought, for in the foreground hundreds of sick, starving people were coming in on foot from the burning road, exhausted; some were wounded, some unable even to walk. Many more stood about the camp, their spent faces staring. There were a number of the large hospital tents, staffed by people from several countries. She knew there were only two doctors among thousands of refugees. She was not a nurse and felt frightened by her own inadequacy in the presence of such tragedy.

Marie Eitz, recruiting volunteers in the United States, had pressed her "You must come, Joan," she said. Joan told her, "I've done nothing more than be a nurse's aide—in World War II at that." But Marie was a determined motivator. She had come to the states to buy trucks, water purifiers, and medical supplies. Joan knew Marie's history. A refugee from Hitler's Germany, Marie would spend all her life helping other refugees. Joan agreed to go for two months.

When she left, her daughter Joanie gave her a few hundred dollars. She asked, "What am I going to do with this? I'll never spend it." She could give it to these people, one by one, as they came into the camp, but they couldn't spend it either. They had more immediate needs than money. "You'll find some use for it," Joanie had said.

The truck had let her out at the American tent, where tattered children lay on the stones waiting to be admitted to the hospital. She glimpsed a child's half-shut eyes, the rapid movement of breath under nearly transparent ribs, as she stepped into the tent. It was dark inside after the brilliant sun; then agonized faces emerged from the darkness. Women and men were shrunken by hunger. She heard their anguished cries. She knew that many people had been tortured.

Overhead signs indicated the rows—A, B, C, D. At the end of row D, which clearly held the most critical cases, she found the head nurse working at a crib that held four starving infants. What could she do here? She knew she couldn't help with the dying babies. Extremely busy, the nurse merely lifted her chin toward the back of the tent and said to Joan, "Do you sew?"

And so she had joined Rosemary. They were making sarongs for the little girls and shorts for the boys. Most of the children were wearing rags when they arrived at the camp.

Many of the women were caring for several sick children. Rosemary said, "The Cambodians take care of all children as if they were their own. If they see a lost child, they take it over, no talking about it." On row A a boy of four or five was fashioning a wagon out of a discarded tin can for his younger sister, who was chattering to him in delight. "These children are like no others," Rosemary said. "As soon as they get some food in them, they have to play."

The children made up games, invented their own toys. Joan loved to watch them as they recovered and slowly learned to smile again. As soon as she and Rosemary finished a garment, they would find the child for it. There seemed to be no end to the need for clothing, just as there seemed to be no end to the lines of those entering the camp.

While the Thai girl Nini was sitting with them, Joan heard a strain of music and asked Rosemary about it. "Before these people left Cambodia, anybody who taught anything was shot," Rosemary said, "so they pretended dumb until they got to the camp. Now they have a school. You should watch them dance."

Nini leaped up and beckoned to Joan, "Come and see."

They walked outside. A quarter of a mile away, beyond some of the other hospital tents, a platform was being constructed. "For dancing," Nini said. Nearby, several Cambodian teachers were training children to dance, with precise movements of their feet, hands, even their fingernails.

Some of the percussion instruments and the gamelan were very heavy. Nini said that the old men—fathers and grandfathers—who played the instruments brought them on foot across the border. They had walked with them for hundreds of miles at a time when music could not have been uppermost in their minds. And now, with the dance teachers, they were forming a company and would soon give performances for all the people in the camp.

Joan noticed that several women were making costumes for the dancers, sewing by hand with small, quick fingers. Many children who were watching the dancers and the dancers themselves needed clothing.

Suddenly she had an idea. "Do you think we could buy a sewing machine in town? I have some money that Joanie gave me."

Nini's face lighted up. She knew a man who could get in touch with the sewing-machine distributor. She needed only to take Joan's ID, her passport, to the dealer.

They went back to the tent, and Joan told Rosemary the plan and asked her what she thought of it. Rosemary nodded. That's the way they do things here. Nini left the tent and returned with a companion, a man who spoke no English but nodded yes, he could arrange everything. Joan gave him her passport, and he disappeared.

She never saw him again. After a day or so, a panic rose in her. People would give an arm and a leg here for an American passport. She and Rosemary endured several days of mounting paranoia. They had no idea even of how to find Nini. They continued to sew by hand, and Joan began to wonder how she would ever get home. After a week, Nini reappeared—with her passport. Her mysterious friend had arranged everything. She and Joan could go and buy the sewing machine.

Nini drove the truck over the bumpy road into the town of Aranyaprathet and through the narrow, crowded streets.

Nini pulled up just beyond a little hole-in-the-wall shop. She said, "You hide here; they charge you much money. I take care of everything."

Joan gave her the money, and the girl's eyes widened as she looked at it. Joan thought of the women who were sewing costumes by hand for the dancers. She asked, "Do you think we could get two?"

"Two? Two machines!" Urging Joan to slide down in the truck seat so that the dealer wouldn't see her, Nini disappeared.

She could hear Nini haggling inside the shop. Very shortly Nini came out, followed by an excited little man who helped her load the machines—yes, *two* machines—onto the truck. They tied them very securely with good strong ropes. The man looked overjoyed as he waved good-bye. Two machines! Probably his biggest sale in years.

Nini drove the truck up to the dancing pavilion, which was nearing completion now. The teachers swarmed about them—they were strong women—and started to untie the machines in great excitement. Men came and took both machines inside the tent amid screams of joy.

"They say it's just what they need," Nini explained, "to make costumes for their dancers."

Joan started to speak—it was what she and Rosemary needed too—but in the face of such delight, she was silent.

Everyone was eager to see the dancers' performance, and the machines hastened it along. The women soon created brilliant costumes. At a dress rehearsal Joan and Rosemary stood on tiptoe on a plank at the rear of the tent. The refugees crowded into the tent, two hundred at a time, to enjoy the glorious dancing.

She and Rosemary went on sewing by hand. She loved the sewing and the beautiful soft-skinned children. She knew she had come for a good reason.

When Joan's two months were up, the truck bumped away from the camp. Tears streamed down her face for many miles at leaving those tender, wounded inventive children she would not see again.

Tish Sommers

Born September 8, 1914   Died October 18, 1985

Born Letetia Innes in Cambria, California, Tish Sommers wanted to study dance in her early years. At eighteen she went to Dresden, Germany, where the great dancer Mary Wigman inspired her. There she found her personal meeting place of art and politics. That was in the early 1930s, during Hitler's rise to power, and the family with whom she lived was Jewish. The ordeal of that family became an initiation into activism for Tish. Ever since those days she has been engaged politically, and for most of her working life as an unpaid volunteer.

When she returned to the states, she organized a dance company for teenagers of the Los Angeles barrio. In the years that followed she worked in Birmingham, Alabama, during the civil rights movement, and in other communities where, for twenty-three years of marriage, her husband's career took her. She raised an adopted child, a son, with whom she has a lasting friendship. Divorced in 1971, after what she describes as a good marriage,

she came to a sharp recognition of a problem touching millions of older women. She had neither Social Security benefits nor medical insurance. For Tish Sommers that was the beginning of her greatest activity.

"Displaced homemakers" became a term of her coinage when, with Laurie Shields, a widow, she formed the Displaced Homemakers Alliance. They worked on an educational fund for older women and persuaded California lawmakers to establish a center for training older women to reenter the job market. Tish was awarded the first Distinguished Service-to-Women Award by the National Commission on Working Women. In 1980 she founded the Older Women's League, OWL, which has since grown to have eighty-six chapters and nearly 12,000 members and provides a voice for older women in all the states. With national headquarters in Washington, D.C., OWL's wisdom is heard wherever public policy is made.

CARE-GIVING

"**W**hat would *you* do if your mother couldn't get the care she needs?" Tish Sommers asked a group of young advertising men and women at the Young & Rubicam agency. The staff had been under orders to find a nonprofit project for Y & R's sixtieth anniversary in 1982, and Tish Sommers gave them not only the public service organization they wanted but a lift of consciousness as well. *Their* mothers without Social Security or Medicare and uncared for if they became chronic invalids? Tish had hit home. She got down to what she wanted for OWL: magazine advertising, some radio time, maybe even television spots. She had only a $25,000 grant from the Rockefeller Foundation for this, but she got all three. The account executives became dedicated not only to the justice of OWL's cause but to the dynamic force for good that is Tish Sommers.

The enthusiasm of older women for Tish's cause is understandable: it is their own. But young people, both men and women, are ignited by her combination of qualities, disarming sweetness, generosity of spirit, and ferocious determination. One admirer described her as "sugar-coated iron."

Sky Halberg, a young woman from the agency, went with her to New York to show their campaign to magazine publishers, and again Tish won over many younger executives, men and women. The ads appeared in *Time* and *Woman's Day,* and also in *Modern Maturity.* OWL was on its way to making a national impact.

Tish's secret may lie in the power she has to remind the young as well as people her own age of their basic human values. Sky Halberg said, "She has renewed and inspired my life. Where before my days were filled with salad dressing and dog food, she got me into a job that involves something that matters deeply to me." She challenges people to stretch themselves. "I used to be scared of making public speeches," said Sky, who went on to become the West Coast manager of Young & Rubicam. "She made me stand up at the national OWL convention to make a presentation. That gave me tremendous confidence. There's nothing I wouldn't do for Tish."

Many others feel the same. Tracy Geary, a young woman from a wealthy family, who in her early thirties started The Women's Foundation, helps with large-gift funding for OWL. Kathy Kelly, a social worker at the Family Survival Project in Oakland, which provides respite care for adults with neurological problems like Alzheimer's disease, speaks of Tish's success in dealing with intergenerational issues. "She's great not only on the age question; she can also inspire different personalities from all age groups." Linden Berry was working at Levi Strauss when Tish came into her life with a small grant from the Levi Strauss Foundation. Tish wanted the masthead for the *OWL Observer,* the monthly newsletter, redesigned. Shortly after helping with that project, Linden decided to devote part of her professional time to working for nonprofit organizations. Tish Sommers hired her for a number of projects. She works on direct mail and has chaired a big fundraising event attended by Jane Fonda, who had also become a Tish enthusiast.

Linden Berry said, "The influence of Tish on younger women—well, it isn't that we're saying 'I wish my mother were like you'; it's more that she's an inspiration in our own lives: 'If you can do what you do with *your* life, I know I can do more than I realize.'

"If you work in a corporation, you can't be compassionate because that's just not what you see in a corporate setting. For instance, if an employee came to me saying she needed time off to move because she and her lover had split up and she was upset, I

couldn't give it to her. The men over me wouldn't see the need—maybe they couldn't feel as affected as she by such things in the first place. I think people look at Tish and think, I want to try harder to bring humanity back into the work I'm in."

Linden sees plenty of humanity at the OWL offices, which occupy the first floor of a large old house in Oakland, space which Tish shares with other women. Among them is Laurie Shields, OWL's executive director, who teamed up with Tish to organize the Displaced Homemakers Alliance and who authored the book *Displaced Homemaker*. The household itself is a living demonstration of one of OWL's programs: shared housing for elders. OWL's work is accomplished in an atmosphere of cheerful cooperation. Volunteer and staff desks are surrounded by stacks of leaflets, flyers, and *OWL Observers*: the women work in such efficiency that coffee is warmed as needed in a microwave oven.

"People who haven't even met Tish often call her with their troubles," Linden Berry says. "Their friends will suggest that they should talk to Tish. Maybe it'll be a woman who had cancer, and Tish will sit there and listen. She'll ask what the woman feels now, what she did when the cancer started spreading, and try to get her onto a positive track. By the time the person gets around to saying, 'Well, who are you and how do you know so much about this?' she's already a couple steps away from where she was before she called."

Tish is well informed about cancer; it is an old enemy of hers. She had beaten it down in her forties, but just as she was beginning to organize OWL, it recurred, reminding her of her sustaining motto: "Organize, don't agonize." Tish had no time for agony at all. She was determined to complete the work she had begun.

She found she could use the same approach in dealing with her illness that she uses in every other aspect of her life. She would stay active and fight it actively. That involved speaking openly about it. "I think this is the kind of thing we have to bring out. There are two ways of treating something that happens in your life, one is passively, one is actively; and when it is something in the medical field, a patient is pretty much in a passive role." She formed a support group of cancer patients, who have been meeting for more than five years. They share everything with one another, from techniques of visualization to medical news. "Don't let me give you the impression it's all cheer. Individually and together we face periods of depression and confusion. I think the key is to recognize that cancer is not a one-time thing." As in her political life, "there's a constant tension and involvement to pull up positive strengths toward living." As a fourth-stage cancer patient, Tish has learned that doctors don't have all the answers in terms of dialogue, and certainly not in terms of treatment. "If you want to stay alive and if you have a lot of things you want to do, you had better become a member of the medical team and learn to make your own decisions. Of course, that goes for the rest of your life if you don't want to end up attached to a lot of tubes beyond the time your life has meaning to you."

She spoke of Agnes DeMille, who had inspired her as a dancer, and who after recovering from a massive stroke taught her body to relearn movement so that she could go back to work. Using a visualization tape, Tish works rigorously on a daily schedule, with as much dedication as one who is training for the Olympics. "I strongly believe in the ability of the mind to influence the immune system and to fight back against illness. The work I do with OWL is competitive with my effort to try to stay healthy. Both take an enormous amount of time, but both contribute to my health." One fight supports the other, and everything about Tish Sommers reflects that integral unity. The young dancer who learned of the inseparability of art and politics has survived with the knowledge that completeness in life must also include an understanding of impermanence and an unflinching recognition of one's own death.

On her way to discuss a fundraiser with Jane Fonda, she became ill, and Fonda insisted on caring for Tish until she recovered. It wasn't long before she was back on her feet. Fonda, another young woman who admires the strength of those who function well in later years, said: "What a tough lady! The only other person I have ever met who is as dedicated as she is to her work is Katharine Hepburn."

Working with illness has made Tish and her associates forcibly aware of a serious shortcoming of the Medicare program—its support is primarily for acute conditions rather than for the chronic illnesses that more commonly plague the elderly. Laurie Shields is coordinating another book project, *Women Take Care*, a collaboration by an OWL group. Research and writing for the book will be done by many women who perform home health care for elders, usually a relative of the elder person and usually without compensation. OWL wants to call attention to the fact that this is another of many areas where nourishment is left for women to do at the expense of their own lives.

One young woman on the committee, Dorothy Smith, speaks of having to leave her husband and son in Germany, where they were living when both her parents became ill, her father with terminal cancer. Although her brother lived near their parents, she nevertheless yielded to the traditional view of "woman's role" and returned to provide the needed care until her father's death some months later. The experience opened her eyes to the shortcomings of both medicine and the Medicare system and made both her and her mother "feminists for life," she says. Her mother was already a member of OWL; Dorothy joined and just recently made the first public address of her life—in support of legislation for in-home respite care service—at a national OWL meeting she and her mother attended together. OWL has designed a model state bill for such services, the first of which was recently passed in Washington State, and will work throughout the country for Medicare reform that addresses this problem.

"We're working on Mother's Day right now," Tish said, "finding a theme for next year." The last two years OWL has made good use of the holiday. "After all, it's the day they put on for us, so we want to turn it back to them with a word about what we *really* need. 'You may think motherhood is as great as apple pie, but what do you do with Mother when her job is done?' Last year we did a public education campaign on earning-sharing in Social Security, which establishes the Social Security credits between husband and wife jointly so that in case of divorce the woman doesn't go out with a zero balance. This year the target will probably be Medicare cuts, maybe with a Mother's Day card people can send to the President. We get a group of people together and always come up with something better than one person can think of on her own. That's our mode of action. Mother's Day is the project closest to my heart right now!"

INDEX

Other books by Charlotte Painter
WHO MADE THE LAMB
CONFESSION FROM THE MALAGA MADHOUSE
SEEING THINGS
REVELATIONS: DIARIES OF WOMEN (with M.J. Moffat)